A letter to a deist, in answer to several objections against the truth and authority of the scriptures (1677)

Edward Stillingfleet

A letter to a deist, in answer to several objections against the truth and authority of the scriptures

Stillingfleet, Edward, 1635-1699.

Attributed to Edward Stillingfleet. cf. BM.

Advertisement: p. [2]-[9] at end.

[6], 135, [10] p.

London : Printed by W.G. : And are to be sold by M. Pitt ..., 1677.

Arber's Term Cat. I / 268

Wing / S5600

English

Reproduction of the original in the Henry E. Huntington Library and Art Gallery

Early English Books Online (EEBO) Editions

Imagine holding history in your hands.

Now you can. Digitally preserved and previously accessible only through libraries as Early English Books Online, this rare material is now available in single print editions. Thousands of books written between 1475 and 1700 and ranging from religion to astronomy, medicine to music, can be delivered to your doorstep in individual volumes of high-quality historical reproductions.

We have been compiling these historic treasures for more than 70 years. Long before such a thing as "digital" even existed, ProQuest founder Eugene Power began the noble task of preserving the British Museum's collection on microfilm. He then sought out other rare and endangered titles, providing unparalleled access to these works and collaborating with the world's top academic institutions to make them widely available for the first time. This project furthers that original vision.

These texts have now made the full journey -- from their original printing-press versions available only in rare-book rooms to online library access to new single volumes made possible by the partnership between artifact preservation and modern printing technology. A portion of the proceeds from every book sold supports the libraries and institutions that made this collection possible, and that still work to preserve these invaluable treasures passed down through time.

This is history, traveling through time since the dawn of printing to your own personal library.

Initial Proquest EEBO Print Editions collections include:

Early Literature

This comprehensive collection begins with the famous Elizabethan Era that saw such literary giants as Chaucer, Shakespeare and Marlowe, as well as the introduction of the sonnet. Traveling through Jacobean and Restoration literature, the highlight of this series is the Pollard and Redgrave 1475-1640 selection of the rarest works from the English Renaissance.

Early Documents of World History

This collection combines early English perspectives on world history with documentation of Parliament records, royal decrees and military documents that reveal the delicate balance of Church and State in early English government. For social historians, almanacs and calendars offer insight into daily life of common citizens. This exhaustively complete series presents a thorough picture of history through the English Civil War.

Historical Almanacs

Historically, almanacs served a variety of purposes from the more practical, such as planting and harvesting crops and plotting nautical routes, to predicting the future through the movements of the stars. This collection provides a wide range of consecutive years of "almanacks" and calendars that depict a vast array of everyday life as it was several hundred years ago.

Early History of Astronomy & Space

Humankind has studied the skies for centuries, seeking to find our place in the universe. Some of the most important discoveries in the field of astronomy were made in these texts recorded by ancient stargazers, but almost as impactful were the perspectives of those who considered their discoveries to be heresy. Any independent astronomer will find this an invaluable collection of titles arguing the truth of the cosmic system.

Early History of Industry & Science

Acting as a kind of historical Wall Street, this collection of industry manuals and records explores the thriving industries of construction; textile, especially wool and linen; salt; livestock; and many more.

Early English Wit, Poetry & Satire

The power of literary device was never more in its prime than during this period of history, where a wide array of political and religious satire mocked the status quo and poetry called humankind to transcend the rigors of daily life through love, God or principle. This series comments on historical patterns of the human condition that are still visible today.

Early English Drama & Theatre

This collection needs no introduction, combining the works of some of the greatest canonical writers of all time, including many plays composed for royalty such as Queen Elizabeth I and King Edward VI. In addition, this series includes history and criticism of drama, as well as examinations of technique.

Early History of Travel & Geography

Offering a fascinating view into the perception of the world during the sixteenth and seventeenth centuries, this collection includes accounts of Columbus's discovery of the Americas and encompasses most of the Age of Discovery, during which Europeans and their descendants intensively explored and mapped the world. This series is a wealth of information from some the most groundbreaking explorers.

Early Fables & Fairy Tales

This series includes many translations, some illustrated, of some of the most well-known mythologies of today, including Aesop's Fables and English fairy tales, as well as many Greek, Latin and even Oriental parables and criticism and interpretation on the subject.

Early Documents of Language & Linguistics

The evolution of English and foreign languages is documented in these original texts studying and recording early philology from the study of a variety of languages including Greek, Latin and Chinese, as well as multilingual volumes, to current slang and obscure words. Translations from Latin, Hebrew and Aramaic, grammar treatises and even dictionaries and guides to translation make this collection rich in cultures from around the world.

Early History of the Law

With extensive collections of land tenure and business law "forms" in Great Britain, this is a comprehensive resource for all kinds of early English legal precedents from feudal to constitutional law, Jewish and Jesuit law, laws about public finance to food supply and forestry, and even "immoral conditions." An abundance of law dictionaries, philosophy and history and criticism completes this series.

Early History of Kings, Queens and Royalty

This collection includes debates on the divine right of kings, royal statutes and proclamations, and political ballads and songs as related to a number of English kings and queens, with notable concentrations on foreign rulers King Louis IX and King Louis XIV of France, and King Philip II of Spain. Writings on ancient rulers and royal tradition focus on Scottish and Roman kings, Cleopatra and the Biblical kings Nebuchadnezzar and Solomon.

Early History of Love, Marriage & Sex

Human relationships intrigued and baffled thinkers and writers well before the postmodern age of psychology and self-help. Now readers can access the insights and intricacies of Anglo-Saxon interactions in sex and love, marriage and politics, and the truth that lies somewhere in between action and thought.

Early History of Medicine, Health & Disease

This series includes fascinating studies on the human brain from as early as the 16th century, as well as early studies on the physiological effects of tobacco use. Anatomy texts, medical treatises and wound treatment are also discussed, revealing the exponential development of medical theory and practice over more than two hundred years.

Early History of Logic, Science and Math

The "hard sciences" developed exponentially during the 16th and 17th centuries, both relying upon centuries of tradition and adding to the foundation of modern application, as is evidenced by this extensive collection. This is a rich collection of practical mathematics as applied to business, carpentry and geography as well as explorations of mathematical instruments and arithmetic; logic and logicians such as Aristotle and Socrates; and a number of scientific disciplines from natural history to physics.

Early History of Military, War and Weaponry

Any professional or amateur student of war will thrill at the untold riches in this collection of war theory and practice in the early Western World. The Age of Discovery and Enlightenment was also a time of great political and religious unrest, revealed in accounts of conflicts such as the Wars of the Roses.

Early History of Food

This collection combines the commercial aspects of food handling, preservation and supply to the more specific aspects of canning and preserving, meat carving, brewing beer and even candy-making with fruits and flowers, with a large resource of cookery and recipe books. Not to be forgotten is a "the great eater of Kent," a study in food habits.

Early History of Religion

From the beginning of recorded history we have looked to the heavens for inspiration and guidance. In these early religious documents, sermons, and pamphlets, we see the spiritual impact on the lives of both royalty and the commoner. We also get insights into a clergy that was growing ever more powerful as a political force. This is one of the world's largest collections of religious works of this type, revealing much about our interpretation of the modern church and spirituality.

Early Social Customs

Social customs, human interaction and leisure are the driving force of any culture. These unique and quirky works give us a glimpse of interesting aspects of day-to-day life as it existed in an earlier time. With books on games, sports, traditions, festivals, and hobbies it is one of the most fascinating collections in the series.

old books. new life.

The BiblioLife Network

This project was made possible in part by the BiblioLife Network (BLN), a project aimed at addressing some of the huge challenges facing book preservationists around the world. The BLN includes libraries, library networks, archives, subject matter experts, online communities and library service providers. We believe every book ever published should be available as a high-quality print reproduction; printed on-demand anywhere in the world. This insures the ongoing accessibility of the content and helps generate sustainable revenue for the libraries and organizations that work to preserve these important materials.

The following book is in the "public domain" and represents an authentic reproduction of the text as printed by the original publisher. While we have attempted to accurately maintain the integrity of the original work, there are sometimes problems with the original work or the micro-film from which the books were digitized. This can result in minor errors in reproduction. Possible imperfections include missing and blurred pages, poor pictures, markings and other reproduction issues beyond our control. Because this work is culturally important, we have made it available as part of our commitment to protecting, preserving, and promoting the world's literature.

GUIDE TO FOLD-OUTS MAPS and OVERSIZED IMAGES

The book you are reading was digitized from microfilm captured over the past thirty to forty years. Years after the creation of the original microfilm, the book was converted to digital files and made available in an online database.

In an online database, page images do not need to conform to the size restrictions found in a printed book. When converting these images back into a printed bound book, the page sizes are standardized in ways that maintain the detail of the original. For large images, such as fold-out maps, the original page image is split into two or more pages

Guidelines used to determine how to split the page image follows:

• Some images are split vertically; large images require vertical and horizontal splits.
• For horizontal splits, the content is split left to right.
• For vertical splits, the content is split from top to bottom.
• For both vertical and horizontal splits, the image is processed from top left to bottom right.

IMPRIMATUR hic Liber
(cui Titulus , *A Letter to a*
DEIST.).

Feb. 8.
1676.

Guil. Jane, R. P. D. *Henr.*
Episc. Lond. *a Sacris*
Domest.

A

LETTER

TO A

DEIST,

In Anſwer to ſeveral

OBJECTIONS

AGAINST THE

TRUTH and *AUTHORITY*

OF THE

Scriptures.

By Bp Stillingfleet

LONDON,

Printed by *W. G.* and are to be ſold by *M. Pitt*,
at the *Angel* in St. *Paul's* Church-Yard, 1677.

THE
PREFACE.

THis *following Discourse was Written for the satisfaction of a particular Person, who* owned *the* Being *and* Providence *of* God, *but expressed a mean Esteem of the* Scriptures, *and the* Christian Religion. *Which is become so common a* Theme *among the* Scepticks *of this* Age, *that the* Author *of this* Discourse *thought it worth his time and care, to consider the force of the Objections that were made against them. Especially, being written in a grave and serious manner, and not with that* Raillery *and* Buffonry, *which the* rude Persons *of this* Age *commonly bestow upon* Religion. *It might be*

A 3   justly

justly expected from such who pretend to Breeding and Civility, that they would at least shew more respect to a thing, which hath prevailed so much among Men of the best Understanding and Education, and who have had no Interest to carry on by it. For it is against the ordinary Rules of Conversation, to affront that which others think they have great Reason to esteem and love; and they would not endure that scorn and contempt of their meanest Servant, which they too often shew towards Religion, and the things belonging to it. If they are not in earnest when they scoff and mock at sacred things, their own consciences will tell them it is a horrible impiety; if they are in earnest, let them debate these things calmly and seriously, and let the stronger Reason prevail. Men may speak sharply and wittily against the clearest things in the World, as the Scepticks

of

of old did against all Certainty of Sense and Reason; but we should think that Man out of his senses, that would now dispute the Being of the Sun, or the Colour of the Snow. We do not say, the Matters of Religion are capable of the same evidence with that of Sense; but it is a great part of judgment and understanding, to know the proportion and fitness of evidence to the Nature of the thing to be proved. They would not have the Eye to judge of tasts, nor the Nose of Metaphysicks; and yet these would be as proper as to have the senses judge of Immaterial Beings. If we do not give as good Reason for the Principles of our Religion, as the nature of Religion considered, can be given for it, let us then be blamed for our weakness in defending it; but let not Religion suffer, till they are sure nothing more can be said for it.

There

The Preface.

Tractat. Theol.
politic.

There is a late Author, I hear is mightily in vogue among many, who cry up any thing on the Atheistical side, though never so weak and trifling. It were no difficult task to lay open the false Reasonings, and inconsistent Hypotheses of his Book; which hath been sufficiently done already in that Language wherein it was written. But if for the Advancement of Irreligion among us, that Book be, as it is talked, Translated into our Tongue, there will not, I hope, want those who will be as ready to defend Religion *and* Morality, *as others are to decry and despise them.*

A Letter of Resolution to a Person unsatisfied about the Truth and Authority of the Scriptures.

SIR,

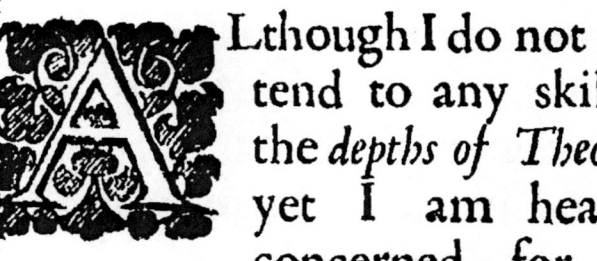Lthough I do not pre-tend to any skill in the *depths of Theology*, yet I am heartily concerned for the *Truth* and *Honour* of the *Christian Religion*; which it is the defign of your papers to undermine. When I firft looked them over, I could not think them fo confiderable as to deferve a particular Anfwer; efpecially, from one in my circumftances, who have fo much

B　　other

other bufinefs lying upon me, and
fo little leifure and health to per-
form it; but I found at the con-
clufion of your Papers, fo earneft
and vehement a defire expreffed
by you, that I would return an
Anfwer, in order to the fettle-
ment of your mind, that I could
not refufe an Office of fo great
Charity, as you reprefent it to be.
I confefs, when I confidered the
nature of your Objections, and
the manner of managing them,
I could hardly believe that they
proceeded from a doubtful Mind,
that was defirous of any fatisfaction; but fince you tell me fo,
I will firft fhew my Charity in be-
lieving it, and then in endeavou-
ring to give you my poor affi
ftance, and impartial advice, in or
der to your fatisfaction. And i
truth, I think impartial advice wil
con

contribute more to that end, than spending Time and Paper in running through all the difficulties, which it is poffible for a cavilling Mind to raife againft the plaineft *Truths* in the World. For there is nothing fo clear and evident, but a *Sophiftical Wit* will always find fomething to fay againft it; and if you be the *Perfon* I take you for, you very well know, that there have been fome, who wanted neither Wit, nor Eloquence, who have gone about to prove, *That there was Nothing in the World; and that if there were any thing, it could not be underftood by Men; that if it were underftood by one Man, it could not be expreffed to another:* And befides fuch extravagant undertakers as thefe, how many have there been, who with plaufible and fubtle Argu-

B 2   ments,

ments, have endeavoured to overthrow all manner of *Certainty*,
either by *Sense* or *Reason*? Must
we therefore quit all pretences to
Certainty, because we cannot, it
may be, Answer all the Subtilties
of the *Scepticks*? And therefore
I am by no means satisfied with
your manner of proceeding,
desiring all particular difficulties to be
Answer'd, before we consider the main
evidences of the Christian Faith :
For the only reasonable way o
proceeding in this matter, is to
consider, first, whether there be
sufficient *Motives* to perswade you
to imbrace the *Christian Faith;*
and then to weigh the difficulties,
and to compare them with the
Reasons and *Arguments* for belie-
ving; and if those do not appear
great enough to overthrow the
force of the other, you may rest
satisfied

satisfied in the *Christian Faith*, although you cannot Answer every difficulty that may be raised against the *Books* wherein our Religion is contained. I pray Sir, consider with your self; do not you think it possible for any man to have Faith enough to save him, unless he can solve all the difficulties in *Chronologie* that are in the *Bible*, unless he can give an account of every particular *Law* and *Custom* among the *Jews*, unless he can make out all the *Prophetick Schemes*, and can tell what the *Number* of the *Beast* in the *Apocalypse* means ? If a Man may believe and be saved, without these things, to what purpose are they objected for the overthrow of the *Christian Faith* ? Do you think a Man hath not reason enough to believe there is *extended*

Matter

Matter in the World , unless he can solve all the difficulties that arise from the *extension* or *divisibility* of *Matter*; or that he hath a *Soul* , unless he can make it clear how an immaterial and material Substance can be so united as our *Soul* and *Body* are? Or that the *Sun* shines, unless he can demonstrate whether the *Sun* or the *Earth* moves? Or that we have any *certainty* of things , unless he can assign the undoubted *criterion* of *Truth* and *Falshood* in all things? These things I mention on purpose , to let you see, that the most certain things , have difficulties about them , which no one thinks it necessary for him to Answer, in order to his assurance of the *Truth* of the *things* ; but as long as the evidence for them is much more considerable than the

Objections

Objections against them, we may safely acquiesce in our assent to them, and leave the unfolding these difficulties to *the Disputers of this World*, or the *Knowledge* of another. Is it not far more reasonable for us to think, that in *Books* of so great *Antiquity*, as those of *Moses* are, written in a Language whose *Idiotisms* are so different from ours, there may be some difficulty in the *Phrases*, or computation of Times or Customs of the People, that we cannot well understand, than that all the Miracles wrought by *Moses* should have been Impostures; and that Law, which was preserved so constantly, maintained with that resolution by the wisest of the People of the *Jews*, who chose to dye rather than disown it, should be

B 4   all

all a cheat? Is it not more reasonable for us to suspect our own Understandings, as to the *Speeches* and *Actions* of some of the *Prophets*, than to think that Men who designed so much the advancing Virtue, and discouraging Vice, should be a pack of Hypocrites and Deceivers? Can any Man of common sense suspect the *Christian Religion* to be a *Fourb*, or an Imposture, because he cannot understand the Number of the *Beast*, or Interpret the *Apocalyptick Visions*? I could hardly have believed any Man pretending to *Reason*, could object these things, unless I saw them, and were called upon to Answer them.

Therefore, Sir, my serious and impartial advice to you is, in the first place to consider and debate

bate the main point, *i. e.* the proofs of the *Christian Doctrin*, and not to hunt up and down the *Scriptures* for every thing that seems a difficulty to you, and then by heaping all these together to make the *Scriptures* seem a confused heap of indigested stuff, which being taken in pieces and considered, with that modesty, diligence, and care, that doth become us, will appear to contain nothing unbecoming that *Sacred* and *Venerable* Name which the *Scriptures* do bear among us.

If therefore, you design not cavilling but satisfaction, you will joyn issue with me upon the most material point, *viz. Whether the Christian Religion were from God, or from Men?* For if this be proved to have been from *God*, all the other things will easily fall

off

off of themselves, or be removed with a little industry.

In the Debate of this, I shall consider, first, what things are agreed upon between us, and then wherein the difference lies.

1. *You grant an absolutely perfect and independent Being, whom we call God.*

2. *That the World was at first Created, and is still governed by Him.*

3. *That He is so Holy, as to be the Author of no Sin, although he doth not hinder Men from sinning.*

4. *That this God is to receive from us all Worship proper to Him, of Prayers, Praises, &c.*

5. *That it is the Will of this God, that we should lead holy, peaceable, and innocent Lives.*

6. *That God will accept mens sincere*

cere Repentance and hearty endeavours to do his Will, although they do not perfectly obey it.

7. That there is a State of Rewards and Punishments in another World, according to the course of Mens Lives here.

8. That there are many excellent Precepts in the writings of the New Testament inducing to Humility and Selfdenyal, and to the Honour of God, and civil duty and honesty of Life; and these in a more plentiful manner than is to be found in any other Profession of Religion publickly known.

The Questions then remaining, are, (1) Whether the matters of Fact are true, which are reported in the Writings of the New Testament? (2) Supposing them true, Whether they do sufficiently prove the Doctrin to have been from God?   1. Whe-

1. *Whether the matters of Fact were true or no?* And as to this point, I wish you had set down the Reasons of your doubting, more clearly and distinctly than you have done : What I can pick up, amounts to these things.

1. *That there can be no certainty of a matter done at such a distance of time, there having been many fictitious Histories in the World.* 2. *That it is probable, that these things might be written, when there was no one Living to detect the falshood of them;* and thus you say, the Grecians, Romans, Egyptians, and other Nations were at first imposed upon by some Men, who pretended to deliver to them the History of their Gods and Heroes, and the Wonders wrought by them. 3. *That these things might more easily be done, before Printing was used;* and that there is reason to

suspect

suspect the more, because of the Pious Frauds of the Primitive Christians, and the Legends of the Papists.

4. That there may have been many more Deceptions and Impostures in the way of propagating false Revelations and Miracles than we can now discover.

5. That we ought not to take the Testimony of Scripture, or the Christian Writers in this case, because they may be suspected of partiality; and that the Testimony of Josephus *is suspected by divers learned Men to be fraudulently put in by Christians.*

6. That there are sufficient grounds from the Story it self, and the Objections of Enemies to suspect the truth of it; because of the contradiction and inconsistency of the parts of it; the want of accomplishment of the Promises and Prophecies of it; the obscurity and unintelligibleness of other parts; the defects of the Persons

sons

sons mentioned therein, St. Paul's *oftentation, the jarrs between* Peter *and* Paul, *and* Paul *and* Barnabas. 7. *That from these things you have just cause to doubt the Apostles sincerity, and you think they might have indirect ends in divulging the Miracles recorded in Scripture; and that Men might be contented to suffer, to make themselves heads of a new Sect of Religion, and to rule over the Consciences of Men; and that they had time enough to make a considerable interest before the Persecutions began.*

This is the force of all I can find out, in the several parts of your Papers towards the invalidating the Testimony concerning the *matters* of *fact* reported in the Writings of the New Testament.

In Answer to all these things, I shall shew; 1. That matters

of

of fact done at such a distance of time may have sufficient evidence to oblige Men to believe them. 2. That there is no reason to suspect the Truth of those Matters of fact which are contained in the History of the New Testament. 3. That the *Apostles* gave the greatest testimonies of their Sincerity, that could be expected from them; and that no matters of fact were ever better attested than those which are reported by them; from whence it will follow, That it is not reason but unreasonable *Suspicion* and *Scepticism*, if not willfulness and obstinacy which makes Men to continue to doubt after so great evidence.

1. That we may have such evidence of *Matters* of *Fact* done at such a *distance* of time as may
oblige

oblige us to believe the Truth o them. This we are first to make out, because several of your Objections seem to imply, *That we can have no certainty of such things; because we cannot know what tricks may have been plaid in former times, when it was far more easie to deceive; and that it is confessed, there have been several Frauds of this kind, which have a long time prevailed in the World.* But have not the very same Arguments been used against all *Religion*, by *Atheists*? And if the *Cheats* that have been in *Religion*, have no force against the *Being* of *God*, why should they have any against the *Christian Religion*? And if the common consent of Mankind signifie any thing as to the acknowledgement of a *Deity*, why should not the

Testi-

Testimony of the *Christian Church*, so circumstantiated as it is, be of sufficient strength to receive the Matters of Fact delivered by it? which is all I at present desire. Do we question any of the Stories delivered by the common consent of *Greek* or *Latin Historians*, although we have only the bare Testimony of those Historians for them? And yet your *Objections* would lye against every one of them: How do we know the great prevalency of the *Roman Empire*? was it not delivered by those who belonged to it, and were concerned to make the best of it? What know we, but *thousands* of *Histories* have been lost, that confuted all that we now have concerning the greatness of *Rome*? What know we, but that *Rome* was destroyed

C   by

by *Carthage*, or that *Hanniba[l]*
quite overthrew the *Roman Em[-]*
pire; or that *Çatiline* was one o[f]
the beſt Men in the World, be[-]
cauſe all our preſent Hiſtorie[s]
were written by Men of the
other ſide ? How can we tell bu[t]
that the *Perſians* deſtroyed th[e]
Macedonians, becauſe all our *A[c]*
counts of *Alexanders* Expeditio[n]
are Originally from the *Greeks*[?]
And why might not we ſuſpe[ct]
greater partiality in all theſe Ca[-]
ſes, when the Writers did not giv[e]
a thouſand part of that evidenc[e]
for their fidelity, that the Fir[ſt]
Chriſtians did ? And yet, wha[t]
ſhould we think of ſuch a perſo[n]
who ſhould call in queſtion th[e]
beſt Hiſtories of all Nations[,]
becauſe they are written by thoſ[e]
of the ſame *Countrey* ? By whic[h]
it ſeems, you will never allo[w]
an[y]

any competent Testimony at all; for if such things be written by Enemies and Strangers, we have reason to suspect both their knowledge and integrity; if written by *Friends*, then though they might know the *Truth*, yet they would write partially of their own side: So that upon this principle, no History at all, ancient or modern is to be believed; for they are all reported either by Friends or Enemies: and so not only Divine, but all Humane Faith will be destroyed. I am by no means a Friend to unreasonable credulity; but I am as little to unreasonable distrust and suspicion; if the one be Folly, the other is Madness. No prudent Man believes any thing, because it is possible to be true; nor rejects any thing meerly because

it

it is poffible to be falfe : But it is the prudence of every Man to weigh and confider all circum- ftances , and according to them, to affent, or diffent. We all know it is poffible for Men to de- ceive, or to be deceived, but we know there is no neceffity o either ; and that there is fuch a thing as Truth in the World ; and though Men may deceive, yet they do not always fo ; and that Men may know they are not de- ceived. For elfe there could be no fuch thing as *Society* among Mankind ; no *Friendfhip*, or *Truft*, or *Confidence* in the Word of ano ther perfon ; becaufe it is poffible that the beft Friend I have ma deceive me, and the World i full of diffimulation , muft therefore believe no Body ? Thi is the juft confequence of thi

wa

way of Arguing, *That we have reason to suspect the Truth of these Matters of Fact, because there have been many Frauds in the World, and might have been many more than we can now discover;* for if this Principle be pursued, it will destroy all Society among Men; which is built on the supposition of mutual trust and confidence that Men have in each other: And although it be possible for all Men to deceive, because we cannot know one anothers hearts, yet there are such Characters of Honesty and Fidelity in some Persons, that others dare venture their Lives and Fortunes upon their Words. And is any Man thought a Fool for doing so? Nay, have not the most prudent and sagacious Men reposed a

C 3   mighty

mighty confidence in the Integrity of others? And without this, no great affairs can be carried on in the World; for since the greateft Perfons need the help of others to manage their bufinefs, they muft truft other Men continually; and every Man puts his Life into the hands of others, to whom he gives any freedome of accefs, and efpecially his Servants: Muft a Man therefore live in continual fufpicion and jealoufie, becaufe it is poffible he may be deceived? But if this be thought unreafonable, then we gain thus much, that notwithftanding the poffibility of deception, Men may be trufted in fome cafes, and their Fidelity fafely relied upon: This being granted, we are to enquire what that affurance is which makes us truft truſt any one ; and whereever we find a concurrence of the ſame circumſtances, or equal evidence of fidelity, we may repoſe the ſame truſt or confidence in them. And we may ſoon find that it is not any ones bare Word that makes us truſt him ; but either the reputation of his Integrity among diſcerning Men ; or our long experience and obſervation of him : This latter is only confined to our own tryal ; but the former is more general, and reaches beyond our own Age, ſince we may have the *Teſtimony* of diſcerning Perſons convey'd down to us in as certain a manner, as we can know the mind of a *Friend* at a 100 Miles diſtance, *viz.* by Writing. And in this caſe, we deſire no more than to be ſatisfied that thoſe things were writ-

C 4

ten

ten by them; and that they deserved to be believed in what they writ; thus, if any one would be satisfied about the passages o the *Peloponnesian War*, and hath heard that *Thucydides* hath accurately written it, he hath no more to do, than to enquire whether this *Thucydides* were capable of giving a good account of it, and for that, he hears that he was a great and inquisitive Person, that lived in that Age, and knew all the occurrences of it; and when he is satisfied of that, his next enquiry is, whether he may be trusted or no; and for this, he can expect no better satisfaction, than that his History hath been in great reputation for its integrity among the most knowing Persons; but how shall he be sure this was the History, written by

Thucy-

Thucydides, since there have been many counterfeit Writings obtruded upon the World? Besides the consent of learned Men in all Ages since, we may compare the *Testimonies* cited out of it with the History we have, and the Style, with the Character given of *Thucydides*, and the Narrations, with other credible Histories of those Times; and if all these agree, what reason can there be not to rely upon the History of *Thucydides*? All learned Men do acknowledge, that there have been multitudes of fictitious writings, but do they therefore question, whether there are any genuine? Or whether we have not the true *Herodotus*, *Strabo*, or *Pausanias*, because there is a counterfeit *Berosus*, *Manetho*, and *Philo*, set forth by *Annius* of *Viterbo*? Do
any

any suspect whether we have an of the genuin Works of *Cicero*, be cause an *Italian* counterfeited Book *De Consolatione* in his name, Or whether *Cæsars Commentarie* were his own, because it is un certain who Writ the *Alexandria* *War* that is joyned with them? By which we see, that we may not only be certain of the Fideli ty of Persons we converse with but of all things necessary to ou belief of what was done at a great distance of time from th *Testimony* of Writers, notwith standing the many supposititious Writings that have been in th World.

But it may be said, *That all this only relates to meer matters of History, wherein a Man is not much concerned whether they be true or false; but the things we are about are matters that*

at *Mens Salvation* or *Damnation* are
id to depend upon, and therefore
eater evidence fhould be given of
efe, to oblige *Men* to believe them.

To this I anfwer.   1. That
y defign herein, was to prove,
at notwithftanding the poffibi-
y of deception, there may be
fficient ground for a prudent
id firm affent to the Truth of
iings done at as great a diftance
f time, and convey'd after the
ime manner, that the Matters
f Fact reported in the *New Te-*
ament are; and hereby thofe ge-
eral prejudices are fhewed to be
nreafonable: And all that I de-
re from this difcourfe is, that
ou would give an affent of the
ime nature to the Hiftory of the
offel, that you do to *Cæfar*, or
ivy, or *Tacitus*, or any other
icient Hiftorian.   2. As to the
greater

greater obligation to assent,
say it depends upon the evidenc
of Divine Revelation, which i
given by the Matters of Fa
which are delivered to us. An
here give me leave to ask you
1. Whether it be any ways re
pugnant to any conception yo
have of God, for him to mak
use of fallible Men to make
known his Will to the World?
2. Whether those Men, though
supposed to be in themselves fallible, can either deceive, or b
deceived, when God makes
known his Mind to them?
3. Whether on supposition, that
God hath made use of such Persons for this end, those are not
obliged to believe them, who
do not live in the same *Age* with
them? If not, then *God* must
either make no *Revelation* at all,

or

or he muſt make a New one every Age: If they are, then the
obligation lies as much on us
now to believe, as if we had
lived and converſed with thoſe
inſpired Perſons.

2. That there is no reaſon to
ſuſpect the Truth of thoſe Matters of Fact which are reported
in the *New Teſtament*; For ſince
it is univerſally agreed among
Men, that Humane *Teſtimony* is a
ſufficient ground for aſſent, where
there is no poſitive ground for
ſuſpicion; becauſe deceiving and
being deceived, is not the common Intereſt of Mankind; therefore we are to conſider what the
general grounds of *ſuſpicion* are,
and whether any of them do
reach the *Apoſtles Teſtimony*, concerning the Matters of Fact reported by them. And the juſt
grounds

grounds of fufpicion are thefe
1. If the *Perfons* be otherw'
known to be Men of artifice an
cunning, full of tricks and diff
mulation, and that make n
Confcience of fpeaking Truth
fo a Lye tends to their greate
advantage; which is too muc
the *Papifts* cafe in their *Legend*
and *Stories* of *Miracles.* 2. I
they temper and fuit their Sto
and Doctrin to the *Humour* an
Genius of the People, they hoj
to prevail upon, as *Mahomet* di
in encouraging *War* and *Lafciviou*
nefs. 3. If they lay the Scene o
their Story at a mighty diftance
from themfelves, at fuch an Age,
wherein it is impoffible either to
prove, or difprove; which is
the cafe of the *Brachmans*, as to
their *Brahmà*, and their *Veda*;
and was of the *Heathens* as to
their

their Fabulous Deities. 4. If there be any thing contained in the Story, which is repugnant to the moſt authentick Hiſtories of thoſe times; by which means the Impoſtures of *Annius* have been diſcovered. 5. If there be evident contradiction in the Story it ſelf; or any thing repugnant to, or unbecoming the Majeſty, Holineſs, Sincerity, and Conſiſtency of a Divine Revelation; on which account we reject *Fanatick* pretences to *Revelations*. If there were any thing of this nature in the *Writings* of the *New Teſtament*, we might then allow there were ſome ground to ſuſpect the *Truth* of what is contained therein: But I ſhall undertake, by the Grace of God, to defend that there is not any foundation for ſuſpicion as to any one of theſe. 1. As

1. As to the *Persons*, such wh
go about to deceive others, mu
be Men that are versed in busines
and know how to deal wit
Men; and that have some inte
rest already that they have gaine
by other means, before they ca
carry on such a design as to abuse
Mankind, by Lyes and Impostures in *Religion* : Therefore the
Atheists lay the deceiving the
World by *Religion*, to the Charge
of *Politicians* and *Law-givers*, to
Men versed in the practice of
Fraud, such as *Numa*, or *Lycurgus*,
or *Xaca*, or *Mahomet*, such as understood the ways of cajoling
the People; or to *subtle Priests*,
that know how to suit the hopes
and fears of the superstitious multitude; whence came the multitude of Frauds in the *Heathen
Temples* and *Oracles*. But would
any

any Man in the World have pitched upon a few *Fishermen*, and illiterate Persons, to carry on such an intrigue as this ? Men that were rude and unexperienced in the World, and uncapable of dealing in the way of Artifice with one of the common Citiens of *Hierusalem.* When was it ever heard that such Men made such an alteration in the *Religion* of the World, as the Primitive *Christians* did, against the most violent persecutions ? And when they prevailed so much, the common charge still against them was, that they were a company of *Rude, Mean, Obscure, Illiterate, simple Men:* And yet in spight of all the Cunning, and Malice, and Learning, and Strength of their adversaries, they gained ground upon them, and prevailed over

D the

the *Obstinacy* of the *Jews*, an
Wisdom of the *Greeks*. If th
Christian Religion had been a mee
design of the *Apostles* to mak
themselves *Heads* of a new Sect
what had this been but to hav
set the Cunning of twelve, o
thirteen Men, of no Interest
or Reputation, against the *Wi*
dom and *Power* of the whol
World? If they had any *Wisdom*
they would never have under
taken such an impossible desig
as this must appear to them
first view: And if they ha
none, how could they ever ho
to manage it? If their aim wei
only at Reputation, they mig
have thought of thousands
ways more probable, and mo
advantageous than this: If w
suppose Men should be willin
to hazard their Lives for the
Repu

eputations, we may suppose withall such Men to have so uch cunning as not to do it till hey cannot help it; but if they an have Reputation and ease to ether, they had rather have it. will therefore put the Case conerning the only Person that had he advantage of a Learned Eduation among the *Apostles*; *viz.* it. *Paul*, and whom you seem to rike at more than the rest: Is t reasonable to believe, that vhen he was in favour with the *anhedrin*, and was likely to dvance himself by his opposiion to *Christianity*, and had a air prospect of Ease and Honour ogether; he should quit all this, o joyn with such an inconsideable and hated company, as the *hristians* were, only to be one f the *Heads* of a very small

D 2 Num-

Number of Men, and to pur-
chase it at so dear a rate as the
loss of his Friends and Interest,
and running on continual Trou-
bles and Persecutions, to the hazard of his Life? It is possible
for Men that are deceived and
mean honestly to do this; but
it is scarce supposable of a Man
in his Senses that should know
and believe all this to be a *cheat*,
and yet own and embrace it, to so
great disadvantage to himself.
When he could not make himself
so considerable by it, as he might
have been without it. Men
must love *cheating* the World at a
strange rate, that will let go fair
hopes of preferment and ease,
and lead a life of perpetual trou-
ble, and expose themselves to
the utmost hazards, only for the
sake of deluding others. If the

Apostles

postles knew all they said to be
false, and made it so necessary
or all Men to believe what they
said to be true; they were some
f the greatest deceivers which
he World had ever known: But
Men that take pleasure in decei-
ing, make use of many artifi-
es on purpose to catch the silly
multitude; they have all the
rts of Insinuation and Fawning
peeches, fit to draw in the
weakest, and such as love to be
atter'd; but what is there ten-
ing this way in all the Apostles
Writings? How sharply do they
peak to the *Jewish Sanhedrin*, upon
he Murther of Christ? With
what plainness and simplicity do
they go about to perswade Men
to be *Christians*? They barely
ll the Matters of Fact concer-
ng the *Resurrection* of *Christ*,

D 3   and

and say *they were eye-witnesses of it*, and upon the credit of this *Testimony* of theirs, they Preach *Faith* and *Repentance* to *Jews*, and *Gentiles*: Was ever any thing farther from the appearance of Artifice than this was? So that if they were deceivers, they were some of the Subtilest that ever were in the World, because there seems to be so little ground for any suspicion of Fraud; and we cannot easily imagin Persons of their Education, capable of so profound dissimulation and so artificial a Cheat. Besides all this, we are to consider how far such Persons do allow the liberty of *dissimulation* and *artificial Juglings*, especially in *Religion*; we see the *Papists* could not practice these things, without being forced to defend them, by shewing how

ow convenient it is for the Peo-
e to be told ſtrange Stories of
ints, on purpoſe *to nouriſh De-*
tion in them: To which end,
ey ſay, *it ſignifies not much, whe-*
er they were true or no: And with-
l they aſſert the *Lawfulneſs of*
uivocations, and Mental Reſerva-
ins, and doing things, not other-
ſe juſtifiable, for the Honour of
eir Church and Religion; And I
all freely confeſs to you, if I
und any countenance to ſuch
ings as theſe, from the Doctrin
: Practice of the *Apoſtles*, it
ould give me too juſt a ground
r ſuſpicion as to what they de-
er'd. For if they allowed *Equi-*
cations, or *Mental Reſervations*,
w could I poſſibly know what
ey meant by any thing they
id? For that which was neceſ-
ry to make the Propoſition true,

D 4   lay

lay without my reach in the Mind of another; and while they so firmly attested that *Christ was risen from the Dead*, they might understand it of a *Spiritual* or *Mystical Resurrection*; but if they should be found to allow *Lying* or *Cheating for the cause of Religion*, their credit would be gone with me; for how could I be any longer sure of the *Truth* of one Word they said? I should be so far from thinking them *Infallible*, that I could not but suspect them to have a design to deceive me. The first thing therefore we are to look at in Persons who require our belief, is the strictest veracity; if they falter in this, they expose themselves to the suspicion of all but credulous Fools. But we no where find greater plainness and sincerity required,

no

no where more strict and severe prohibitions of dissimulation in *Religion*, nor more general Precepts about *speaking Truth*, than in the Writings of the *New Testament*. *But might not all this be done with the greater artifice to prevent suspicion?* Suspicion is a thing, *which he that set bounds to the Sea*, can set no bounds to; if Men will give way to'it, without reason, there can be no end of it. For the most effectual ways to prevent it, will still afford new matter and occasion for it. If Men do use the utmost means that are possible, to assure others of their sincerity, and they will not believe them, but still suspect the design to be so much deeper laid; there is no way left possible to satisfy such Men; their suspicion is a disease incurable

rable by rational means, and such persons deserve to be given over as past all remedy. If Men act like prudent Men, they will judge according to the *Reason* of *Things*; but if they entertain a jealousie of all Mankind, and the most of those who give them the greatest assurance they have no Intention to deceive them, it is to no purpose to go about to satisfie such Persons, for that very undertaking makes them more suspicious. If the *Apostles* therefore gave as much ground as ever any *Persons* did, or could do, that they had no design to impose upon the World, but proceeding with all the fairness and openness, with the greatest evidence of their sincerity, there can be no reason to fasten upon them the imputation of cunning Men

Men who made it their bufinefs
to deceive others.

2. This will more appear if
we confider the *Matters* deliver'd
by them, and the nature of their
Doctrin. For if the *Chriftian Re-
igion* were only a contrivance of
the firft Preachers of it, it muft
by the event be fuppofed that they
were very fubtle Men, who in fo
little time, and againft fo great
oppofition could prevail over
both *Jews* and *Gentiles* ; but if
we reflect on the *nature* of their
Doctrin, we can never imagin
that thefe Men did proceed by
the fame Methods that Men of
fubtilty do make ufe of. If it
were there own contrivance, it
was in their power to have framed it as they thought fit themfelves; and in all probability, they
would have done it in a way
most

most likely to be successful; but the *Christian Religion* was so far from it, as though they had industriously designed to advance a *Religion* against the *genius* and *inclination* of all Mankind. For it neither gratifies the voluptuous in their Pleasures, nor the Ambitious in their desires of External Pomp and Greatness, nor the Covetous in their thirst after Riches; but lays a severe restraint on all those common and prevailing Passions of Mankind; which *Mahomet* well understood, when he suited his *Religion* to them. *Christianity* was neither accommodated to the Tempe and Genius either of *Jews* or *Gentiles*: The *Jews* were in great expectation of a Temporal *Princ* at that time to deliver them from the *Roman* Slavery; and ever

on

one that would have set up for such a *Messias*, might have had followers enough among them, as we find afterwards by the attempts of *Barchocebas* and others. But the *Messias* of the *Christians* was so directly contrary to their hopes and expectations, being a *poor* and *suffering Prince*, that this set them the more against his Followers, because they were hereby frustrated of their greatest hopes, and defeated in their most pleasing expectations: But besides, if they would have taken in the *Mosaick Law*, it might in probability have succeeded better; but this St. *Paul* would by no means hear of. *But if they rejected the Jews, methinks they should have been willing to have had some assistance from the Gentiles. No, they charged them with*

Idolatry

Idolatry where ever they came, and would not joyn in any parts of their Worſhip with them; nor ſo much as Eat of the *remainder* of their *Sacrifices*. But ſuppoſing they had a mind to ſet up wholly a new *Sect* of their own, yet we ſhould think they ſhould have framed it after the moſt plauſible manner, and left out all things that were moſt liable to Reproach and Infamy: But this they were ſo far from, that the moſt contemptible part of the *Chriſtian Religion*, viz. *A Crucified Saviour*, they inſiſt the moſt upon, and Preach it on all occaſions, and in compariſon of it, ſtrangely deſpiſe all the *Wiſdom* and *Philoſophy* of the *Greeks*. What did theſe Men mean, if *Chriſtianity* had been only a *contrivance* of theirs? If they had but left out

this

this one circumstance, in all Human probability, the excellent moral Precepts in *Christianity* would have been highly magnified among all those who had been bred up under the Instructions of *Philosophers*. Nay, they would not make use of the most commendable Methods of Humane Wisdom; nor do as the *Jesuits* have done in *China*, make Men have a better opinion of the *Religion* they brought, for their skill in *Mathematicks* and *Astronomy*; but as much as it was possible, to let the World see it was no contrivance of Humane Wisdom, they shunned all the ways of shewing it in the manner of its propagation. Nay, when the People would have given the *Apostles* Divine Worship, never were vain Men more concerned

to

to have it, than they to oppose it; And do these things look like the Actions of Men that designed only to make themselves great, by being the *Heads* of a new *Sect* of *Religion* ?

3. Men that made it their design to deceive the World, if they had thought it necessary to bring in any matter of *Story* concerning the *Author* of their *Religion* would have placed it at such *a distance of time*, that it was not capable of being disproved : As it is apparent in the *Heathen Mythologie* ; for the Stories were such, as no person could ever pretend to confute them otherwise than by the inconsistency of them with the common principles of *Religion*. But if we suppose *Christianity* to have been meer device, would the *Apostle* hav

have been so senseless to have laid the main proof of their *Religion* on a thing which was but newly acted, and which they were very capable of enquiring into all the Circumstances that related to it, *viz.* the *Resurrection of Christ from the Dead.* We may see by the whole design of the *New Testament*, the great stress of *Christianity* was laid upon the Truth of this; to this, *Christ* himself appealed before hand : to this all the *Apostles* refer as the mighty confirmation of their Religion; and this they deliver as a thing which themselves had seen, and had conversed with him for 40 Days togeher, with all the demonstratins imaginable of a *true* and *real Body* : And that not to one or two credulous Persons, but so

E   many

many of them who were hard
to be satisfied, and one, not without the moſt ſenſible evidence;
but beſides theſe, they tell us of
500 *at once who ſaw him*, *where of
many were then living* when thoſe
things were written.   Now I
pray tell me what *Religion* in the
World ever put it ſelf upon ſo
fair a tryal as this? Of a plain
Matter of Fact as capable of being atteſted as any could be.
Why did not *Amida*, or *Brahma*,
or *Xaca*, or any other of the
Authors of the preſent *Religion*
of the *Eaſt Indies* ? Why did no
Orpheus, or *Numa*, or any othe
introducers of *Religious* Cuſtom
among the *Greeks* or *Romans* ? O
Mahomet among the *Arabians* pu
the iſſue of the Truth of thei
Religion on ſuch a plain and eaſ
tryal as this ? If you ſay *That Chri*

appear

ppeared only to his *Friends*, *who*
ere ready to believe *such things*, *and*
ot among *his Enemies*: I Anſwer,
That though they were his
riends, yet they were very hard
) be perſwaded of the *truth* of
at firſt; and afterwards gave
arger Teſtimonies of their fide-
ty than the Teſtimony of the
reateſt *Enemies* would have been;
or we ſhould have had only
heir *bare Words* for it, (if they
ould have given that, which
very queſtionable, conſidering
heir dealing with the other *Mi-*
cles of *Chriſt*:) But the *Apoſtles*
anifeſted their *ſincerity* by all
al proofs that could be thought
fficient to ſatisfie Mankind;
pealing to the very Perſons
ho were concerned the moſt in
having a hand in the Death
Chriſt, declaring their grea-

E 2 teſt

test readiness to suffer any thing
rather than deny the Truth of it,
and laying down their Lives at
last for it.   If all this had been
a meer Fiction, how unlikely
is it, that among so many as
were conscious of it, no one
person by hopes or fears, by
flatteries or threatnings, could
ever be prevailed upon to deny
the Truth of it. If there had
been any such thing, what tri-
umphing had there been among
the *Jews* ; and no doubt his name
had been Recorded to Posterity
among the Writers both of *Jew*
and *Gentiles* that were professed
Enemies of *Christianity*. But
they are all wonderfully silent
in this matter ; and instead o
saying enough to overthrow the
truth of Christianity, as you seem
to suggest, I do assure you, I am
mightily

nightily confirmed in the belief
of the Truth of it, by carefully
observing the slightness of the
Objections that were made
against it, by its most professed
enemies.

But you seem to imply, *That
all this Story concerning Christ was
invented long after the pretended time
of his being in the World*, Why
may not you as well suspect, that
Julius Cæsar lived before *Romulus*;
or that *Augustus* lived at the Seige
of *Troy*? For you might as well
eject all History upon such
grounds as those you assign; and
think *Mahomet* as right in his
Chronology, as the *Bible*. It is
time for us to burn all our *Books*,
if we have lived in such a Cheat
all this while. Methinks you
might as well ask, whether *Lu-
retia* were not *Pope Joan*? Or

E 3   *Alexan-*

Alexander the *sixth*, one of the *Roman Emperours* ? Or whether *Luther* were not the *Emperour* of *Turky* ? For there is no greater evidence of any History in the World, than there is, that all the things reported in the *New Te-stament* were done at that time, when they are pretended to be.

4. Therefore we offer this Story of the *New Testament* to be compared with all the *Circumstan-ces of that Age*, delivered by any other *Historians*, to try if any *inconsistencies* can be found therein: Which is the most reasonable way can be taken to disprove any History. If it could be proved, that there could be no such *Taxation* of the *Empire* as is mention'd in the time of *Augu-stus*, that *Herod* did not live in that

that *Age*, or that the *Jews* were not under the *Roman Government*, or that there were no *High Priests* at that time, nor the *Sects* of *Pharisees* and *Saducees*, or that there were any other remarkable *characters* of time set down in the *History* of the *New Testament*, which could be manifestly disproved; there were some pretence to call in Question the Truth of the Story; but there is not the least Foundation for any scruple on this account; All things agreeing so well with the truest accounts we have of that *Age*, both from *Josephus* and the *Roman Historie*. I shall not insist on the particular *Testimony* of *Josephus* concerning *Christ*, because we need it not; and if those who question it, would proceed with the same severity against many

E 4   other

other particular paſſages in good *Authors* , they might as well call them in queſtion as they do that; ſince it is confeſſed , that all the Ancient *Manuſcripts* have it in them , and ſuppoſing that it doth not come in well , muſt we ſuppoſe it impoſſible for *Joſephus* to Write incoherently ? Yet this is the main Argument that ever I have ſeen urged againſt this *Teſtimony* of *Joſephus*. But I ſay, we need it not; all other things concurring in ſo high a degree to prove the *Truth* of the *Hiſtory* of *Chriſt*. Yet ſince you ſeem to expreſs ſo much doubtfulneſs concerning it , *as though it were framed when there was no one living capable of diſproving it* ; give me leave to ſhew you the great abſurdity of ſuch a Suppoſition. 1. Becauſe we have the plain Teſtimonies of the

the greatest Enemies of *Christi-
nity*, that there was such a Person as *Christ* was, who suffered
according to the *Scripture Story*.
For *Tacitus* not only mentions the
Christians as suffering at *Rome* for
their *Religion* in the *time* of *Nero*,
(*Annal.* 15.) but saith, *That the
Author of this Religion was one
Christ, who suffered under* Pontius
Pilate, *Procurator of* Judea, *in
the time of* Tiberius; which is an
irrefragable Testimony of the
Truth of the Story concerning
Christ, in an *Age*, when if it
had been false, nothing could
have been more easily detected
than such a Fiction, by the number of *Jews* which were continu-
lly at *Rome* : And neither *Julian*,
nor *Celsus*, nor *Porphyrie*, nor
Lucian did ever question the *truth*
of the Story it self; but only up-
braided

braided the *Christians* for attributing too much to *Christ*. 2. If there were really such a Person as *Christ* was, who suffered as *Tacitus* saith, then the whole Story could not be a Fiction, but only some part of it; and these additional parts must either be contrived by the *Apostles*, or after their time: Not after their time, for then they must be added after *Christianity* was received in the World, for that, as appears by *Tacitus*, was spread in the *Apostles* times as far as *Rome*; and if these parts were not received with it; the Cheat would presently have been discover'd as soon as broached, by those who had embraced *Christianity* before: And besides, *Tertullian* in his time appeals to the *Authentick Writings* of the *Apostles* themselves, which

were

were then extant, wherein the
same things were contained, that
we now believe: If these things
then were forged, it must be by
the *Apostles* themselves; and I
dare now appeal to you, whether
ever any Story was better capable
of being disproved than this was,
if it had not been true, since it
was published in that very time
and place, where the *Persons*
were living, who were most
concerned to disprove it : As appears by the hatred of the *Jews* to
the *Christians*, both then and ever
since : which is a very observa-
ble circumstance for proving the
truth of *Christian* Religion; for the
Jews and *Christians* agreed in the
Divine Revelations of old, the
Christians believed moreover, that
Christ was the *Messias* promised;
this *Christ* lived and dyed among
the

the *Jews* his Enemies; his *Apostles* Preached, and wrought Miracles among their most inveterate Enemies, which Men that go about to deceive never care to do: And to this Day the *Jews* do not deny the *Matters of Fact*, but look on them as insufficient to prove *Jesus* of *Nazareth* to have been the *Messias*: Nay, *Mahomet* himself, who in all probability would have overthrown the whole Story of the *New Testament*, if he could have done it with any colour, yet speaks very honourably of *Christ* and of the great things which were said and done by him.

5. That there is nothing in the *Christian Religion*, unbecoming the *Majesty*, or *Holiness*, or *Truth* of a *Divine Revelation*. As to th precepts, *you acknowledge their excellency*

ellency; and the *Promises* chiefly
refer either to *Divine Grace*, or
future Glory; And what is there
therein unbecoming *God*? And as
to what concerns the *Truth* of it,
we have as great Characters of
that throughout, as it is possible
for us to expect; there appea-
ring so much simplicity, sincerity, candour, and agreement in
all the parts of it. Some Men
would have been better pleased,
it may be, if it had been all written by one *Person*, and digested
into a more exact method, and
set forth with all the Lights and
Ornaments of Speech. This
would have better become an
invention of Men, but not a
Revelation of *God*: Plainness and
simplicity have a natural greatness above art and subtilty; and
therefore *God* made choice of
                                 many

many to write, and at several times, that by comparing them we may see how far they were from contriving together, and yet how exactly they agree in all things which Men are concerned to believe. But you say, *We have many infirmities of the Apostles discovered therein, their heats and animosities one against another.* But I pray consider; 1. How came you to know these things; Is it not by their own Writings? And if they had been such, who minded only their applause, had it not been as easie to have concealed these things, and would they not certainly have done it, if that had been their aim? If *St.* Paul *seems to boast,* doth he not do it, with that constraint to himself, as a Man that is forced to do it for his own vindication

against

against malicious Enemies? And who ever denyed a Man of a generous mind the liberty of speaking for himself? 2. But suppose *they had infirmities and heats among them*; doth this prove that *God* could not make use of them as his Instruments to declare his *Truth* to the World? Then it will follow, that *God* must never reveal his will by *Men*, but by *Voices* from *Heaven*, or *Angels*, or the *assumption* of the *humane Nature by the Divine*. But, if *God* be not denyed the liberty of imploying meer Men, we cannot find so great evidences of Piety and Zeal, of Humility and Self-denyal, of Patience and Magnanimity, of Innocency and universal Charity in any Men as were in the *Apostles*; And therefore did appear with the

most

most proper *Characters* of *Embassadors* from Heaven. And I dare venture the comparison of them with the best *Philosophers*, as to the greatest and most excellent *virtues*, for which they were the most admired; notwithstanding the mighty difference as to their Education; allowing but the same Truth as to the Story of the *New Testament*, which we yield to *Xenophon*, or *Diogenes Laertius*, or any other Writers concerning them.

But what is it then which you object against the Writings of the *New Testament*, to make them inconsistent with the Wisdom of God? I find but two things in the Papers you sent me. 1. *Want of the continuance of the Power of Miracles, which you say is Promised.* Mark

16.

16. 17. ·2. *The number of the Beast in the Revelations.* But, Good Sir, confider, what it is to call in queftion a Divine Revelation for fuch Objections as thefe are? Muft there be no Revelation, unlefs you underftand every Prophecy, or the extent of every promife? Be not fo injurious to your own Soul, for the fake of fuch Objections, to caft away the great affurance which the *Chriftian Religion* gives us, as to the Pardon of Sin upon Repentance here, and eternal Happinefs in another World. Would you reject all the Writings of *Plato*, becaufe you do no more underftand fome part of his *Timæus* than the number of 666? You muft have a very nice faith, that can bear with no difficulties at all, fo that if there be but

F   one

one or two hard things that you cannot digest, you must throw up all the best Food you have taken, at this rate you must starve your Body, as well as ruin your Soul. But of these places afterwards.

3. I have hitherto removed the grounds of Suspicion, I now come to shew the positive Testimonies of their *Sincerity* which the *Apostles* shewed, which were greater than were ever given to any other Matter of Fact in the *World.* I will then suppose the whole *Truth* of the *Christian Doctrine* to be reduced to this one Matter of Fact, Whether *Christ did rise from the dead or no?* for (as I have said already) it is plain, the *Apostles* put the main force of all that they said upon the *Truth* of this; and often declared, that they were appointed to be the

Witnesses

ítneſſes of this thing. Now
ẗ us conſider how it is poſſible
r Men to give the higheſt aſſu-
nce of their *ſincerity* to others;
d that muſt be either by giving
ẽ utmoſt Teſtimony that Men
ĩn give; or by giving ſome Te-
imony above that of Men,
hich cannot deceive, which is
ẽ *Teſtimony of God.*

1. They gave the *utmoſt Te-*
imony that meer Men could give
f their *fidelity.* I know no bet-
r way we have for a full aſſu-
nce as to any humane Teſtimo-
ỹ, than to conſider what thoſe
ircumſtances are which are
ẽnerally allowed to accompany
ruth, and if we have the con-
ȓrence of all theſe, we have
much as can be expected: For
othing that depends on *Teſti-*
ny can be proved by *Mathema-*

F 2   *tical*

tical Demonstration. But notwith
standing the want of this, eith
we may have sufficient ground t
assent to *Truth* upon *Testimony*,
there can be no difference know
between *Truth* and *Falshood* b
Humane Testimony; which ove
throws all Judicial proceeding
among Men; the *Justice* where
of doth suppose not only t
veracity of *Humane Testimony*; B
that it may be so discerned b
others, that they may safely n
ly upon it. Now the main thin
to be regarded as to the *Truth*
Humane Testimony are these. 1.
Men testifie nothing but wh
they saw. 2. If they testifie
at no long distance of time fro
the thing done. 3. If they n
stifie it plainly, and witho
doubtful expressions. 4. If
great number agree in the sam

Test

Testimony.　5. If they part with all that is valuable to Mankind, rather than deny the Truth of what they have testified; And where all these concur, it is hardly possible to suppose greater evidence to be given of the *Truth* of a *Thing*; and now I shall shew that all these do exactly agree to the *Apostles Testimony* concerning the *Resurrection* of *Christ*.

1. They testified nothing but what they saw themselves. The *Laws* of *Nations* do suppose that greater credit is to be given to the *witnesses* than to any others, hence the Rule in the Civil Law *Testimonium de auditu regulariter non valet:* Because, say the *Civilians* and *Canonists,* *Witnesses are to te-* *stifie the Truth, and not barely the pos-* *sibility of things;* that which Men *see,* they can testifie whether

they

they are or not: That which Men only hear, may be, or not be; and their *Testimony* is not of the *Fact*, but is looked on as more uncertain, and ought to have greater allowances given it; but the Apostles testified only *what they saw and handled*; an that after the most scrupulous en quiry into the *Truth* of *Christ Body*, and after many *doubts an suspicions* among themselves abou it; so that they did not seem ha stily and rashly to believe wha they afterwards declared to th World. Now a *Body* was a pr per object of Sense, and no try al could be greater, or more ac curate than theirs was; nor an satisfaction fuller than puttin their *fingers* into the very *woun* of the *pierced side*.

2. They did not stay till th

circum

circumstances might have slipt out of their Memories, before they testified these things; but very soon after, while the impression of them was fresh upon them: If they had let these Matters alone for any long time, the *Jews* would have asked them presently, if these things were true, why did we not hear of them as soon as they were done? Therefore we see the Apostles on the very day of *Pentecost*, a little after *Christs ascension* to Heaven, openly and boldly declare the *Truth* of these things, not in private corners among a few *Friends*, but in the most solemn meeting of their Nation from all parts; which was the worst time could have been chosen, if they had any intention to deceive.

3. They

3. They testifie it in as *plain a manner* as is possible, on purpose to prevent all mistakes of their meaning, *This Jesus hath God raised up, whereof we all are Witnesses; Therefore let all the House of* Israel *know assuredly, that God hath made that same Jesus, whom ye have crucified, both Lord and Christ.* Men that had a mind to deceive would have used some more general and doubtful words, than these were.

Acts 2. 32. 36.

4. If this had been testified by one single witness, the World would have suspected the Truth of his Testimony; for according to the Rule in the *Civil Law* in the case of *Testimony, Vox unius, vox nullius est*: But this was testified by very many; not meerly by the twelve Apostles, but by 500 at once; among whom some might

might be suppofed to have fo much honefty, or at leaft capable of being perfwaded to have difcovered the Impofture, if they had in the leaft fufpected any.

5. But that which adds the greateft weight to all this, is, that there was not one of all the Apoftles, and fcarce any one of the reft, but expofed themfelves to the utmoft *hazards* and *dangers*, rather than deny or retract the *Truth* of what they witneffed. If the *People* had been carelefs and indifferent about *Religion*, it is poffible Men might have gone on in a Lye fo long till they had gotten *intereft* enough to maintain it; but no fooner did the Apoftles appear, witneffing thefe things, but they met with an early and vigorous oppofition, and that from the chiefeft Men in

Power,

Power, who made it their business to suppress them. Now in this case, they were put to this choice, if they would renounce or conceal the *Truth* of what they testified, they might presently enjoy ease, and it may be, rewards too; but if they went on, they must look for nothing but the sharpest persecution; and this they met with almost in all places; and is it conceivable, that Men should be so *fond* of a *lye*, to forsake all and follow it, and at last to take up their cross for it? If *credit* and *interest* in the hearts of People, might carry a Man on a great way in the delusion, yet he would be loth to dye so it; and yet there was never a on of the Apostles, but ventured hi life for the *Truth* of this; and al but one, they tell us, did suffe

Martyr

Martyrdom for it. I pray, Sir, confider, where you ever meet with any thing like this, that fo many Men fhould fo refolutely dye, for what themfelves at the fame time knew to be a lye; and that they muft certainly do, if it were all a contrivance of their own heads.

2. But although in thefe things they went as high as it was poffible for *humane Teftimony* to go, yet they had fomething beyond all this, which was a *concurrence of a Divine Teftimony*, in the *miraculous gifts* and *operations* of the *Holy Ghoft*. And this we affert to be the higheft Teftimony can be given in the World, of a *Truth* of any thing; becaufe *God* will not employ his *Power* to deceive the World. And as all other *Truth* hath a *criterion* proper

to it; so this seems to be the proper *criterion* of a *Divine Testimony*, that it hath the *power of Miracles* going along with it. For if we do suppose God to make known his Mind to the World, it is very reasonable to believe there should be some *distinguishing note* of what is immediately from God, and what comes only from the *inventions* of *Men*; and what can be more proper to distinguish what comes from *God*, and what from *Men*, than to see those things done which none but *God* can do? But against this you object several things, which I shall easily and briefly Answer.

1. *You cannot tell what it is that Miracles do attest; not all their Doctrin, since* Paul *said, some was not from the Lord.* Answ. *Miracles* do attest the *veracity* of the
Speaker,

Speaker, and by confequence the *truth* of the *Doctrin*; *not that you fhould believe that to be from the Lord, which he faid was not*; but that which he faid, was from the Lord. But when he makes fuch a diftinction himfelf, it is very unreafonable to urge that as an Argument, that he had *nothing from the Lord*; it is much rather an argument of his candor and ingenuity, that he would not pretend to *Divine Revelation*, when he had it not.

2. *You would have it fignified, what Doctrin it is which is attefted by Miracles, fince the Doctrins of Scripture lye in heaps and confufion.* *Anfw.* To what purpofe fhould any Doctrins be fingled out to have the *Seal* of *Miracles* fet to them, fince it is their *Divine Commiffion* to Teach and declare the

the *Will* of *God*, which is *sealed* by it? And what they did so Teach and declare, is easily known by their Writings.

3. *But why do not Miracles still continue? Answ.* Because there are no Persons employ'd to Teach any *new Doctrines*; and no Promise of *Scripture* doth imply any more: For the *signs* which were to follow them that believe, were such as tended to the first confirmation of the *Christian Faith*; which being effected, their use ceased; and so to ask why God doth not continue a Gift of *Miracles* to convince Men that the former were true, is to the same purpose as to ask why *God* doth not make a *New Sun*, to satisfie *Athiests* that he made the *Old*?

4. *But doth not the Scripture say, that wonders are not always to be*
                                    taken

taken as confirmations of the Truth of Doctrin, since false Prophets may work Wonders, Deuteron. 13. 1. Answ. That signifies no more, than that Wonders are not to be believed against the Principles of Natural Religion; or Revealed Religion already confirmed by greater Miracles: And that those who would value such a particular sign above all the series of Miracles their Religion was first established by, may be justly left to their own delusions. You might as well object the lying Wonders of the Man of Sin, against all the Miracles of Christ and his Apostles. If God hath once done enough to convince Men, he may afterwards justly leave them to the tryal of their Ingenuity; as a Father, that hath used great care to make his Son understand

true

true Coyn, may afterwards suffer *false* to be laid before him, to try whether he will mind his being cheated or no?

5. But you may yet farther demand, *what the Testimony of Miracles doth signifie to the Writings of the New Testament? Answ.* 1. The Miracles do sufficiently prove the *Authority* of that Doctrin, which was delivered by those who wrought *Miracles*; as *Christ* and his *Apostles*. 2. If there had been the least ground to question the *Truth* and *Authority* of these *Writings*, they had never been so universally received in those *Ages*, when so many were concerned to enquire into the *Truth* of these things; for we see several of the *Books* were a long time examined, and at last, when no sufficient reason could

be

be brought againſt them, they were received by thoſe *Churches*, which at firſt ſcrupled the receiving them: And I am ſo far from thinking the *doubts* of the firſt *Ages* any Argument againſt the *Authority* of a *Book*, that by the objections of ſome againſt ſome of them, I am thereby aſſured, that they did not preſently receive any *Book*, becauſe it went under the name of an *Apoſtolical Writing*: As I am the more confirmed in the belief of the *Reſurrection* of *Chriſt*, becauſe ſome of the *Diſciples* were at firſt very *doubtful* about it.

6. You may yet ask, *What doth all this ſignifie to the Writings of the Old Teſtament, which were written at a longer diſtance of Time from us, and in a more Ignorant Age of of the World?* Anſw. There can-

not

not be a *more* evident proof of the *Old Testament*, than by the *New*: For if the *New* be *true*, the *Old* must be so, which was confirmed so plainly and evidently by it; our *Saviour* and his *Apostles* appealing to *Moses* and the *Prophets* on all occasions. So that the same *Miracles* which prove their *Testimony* true, do at the same time prove the *Divine Authority* of the *Old Testament*, since it is so expresly said in the *New*, *That Holy Men of God did speak as they were moved by the Holy Ghost.*

But after all this, You urge, that you have discover'd such things in these Writings as could not come from God, as

    1. Contradictions in them. 2. Some things inconsistent with the Wisdom of God. 3. Promises made that were never fulfilled. 4. Things so obscure

43

s no one can tell the meaning of them.
Under these four Heads I shall
examin the particular allegations
you bring against the *Scriptures*.

1. Under the head of *Contra-*
dictions, you insist on the *Prophecy*
Gen. 15. 13, 14, 15, 16. *made to*
Abraham concerning his Posterity;
compared with the Accomplishment
mentioned, Exod. 12. 40. 41.
and the force of your Argument
lyes in this, That the Prophecy in
Genesis doth imply that the Servitude
of the Children of Israel *in* Egypt
was to be 40 *Years*; *or* 430 *saith*
Exod. but both these are repugnant
to other places of Scripture, which
make their abode in Egypt *not to*
exceed 215 *Years*; *or at the highest,*
by the number of Generations could
not exceed 350 *Years, stretching*
them to the utmost advantage. To
this which you lay so much

weight

weight upon, I Answer distinctly,

1. By your own confession, supposing the 430 Years to begin from the *Covenant* made with *Abraham*, the accomplishment mentioned, *Exod.* 12. 40. doth fall out exactly in the time of the *Children* of *Israels* going out of *Egypt*, for you have proved from *Scripture*, that from the *Covenant* with *Abraham* to *Jacobs* being in *Egypt*, were 215 Years; to which you add, *that* Coath *being supposed 5 Years Old at the going into* Egypt; *and that at 70 Years he Begat* Amram, *and that* Amram *at at 70 Begat* Moses, *to which* Moses *his 80 Years being added, makes up the other 215 Years, whereby we have the full 430 Years, by your own computation.* Now, Sir, I pray consider what reason you have

to

to charge the *Scripture* with contradiction in a Matter your self acknowledges, so exactly accomplished in this way of computation?

2. But you say, *the Words will not bear this; because they speak of the 400 Years to expire in their Servitude in* Egypt. *Answ.* For this we must consider the importance of the Words both in *Genesis* and *Exodus.* There is not a Word of *Egypt* mentioned in *Genesis*; but only in general it is said, *Thy Seed shall be a Stranger in the Land that is not theirs, and shall serve them, and they shall afflict them* 400 *Years*; and it will conduce very much to the right understanding this Prophecy to consider the main scope and design of it, which was not to tell *Abraham* how long they should be in *servitude* to the Egyp-

tians,

tians, but how long it would be before his Seed fhould come to the *poffeffion* of the promifed *Land*; And it feems *Abraham* by the *Queftion*, Gen. 15. 7. 8. did expect to have the Inheritance of this Land *in his own time*: To this therefore *God* Anfwers, by telling him, he meant no fuch thing, but it was intended for *his Seed*, and that not fuddenly neither, for they were to tarry *till the iniquity of* the Amorites *fhould be full*, which would not be till the *fourth* Generation; and then *his Seed fhould after* 400 *Years*, come to the *Poffeffion of the Promifed Land*; *but in the mean time they were to Sojourn in a Land that was not theirs, and to meet with many hardfhips and difficulties*. This is plainly the fcope of this *prophecy*, and by attending to it, the great Objections

presently

resently appear without force; or the *Land* of *Canaan* notwithstanding the Promise, was by the *Patriarchs* themselves looked on as a *Land* wherein they were *strangers.* So *Abraham* saith *Gen.* 3. 4. *I am a Stranger and a Sojurner with you;* and which is more remarkable in the blessing of *Jacob* by *Isaac*, to whom the *Promise* was made, it is said; *And give thee the Blessing of Abraam to thee, and to thy Seed, that thou mayest inherit the Land wherein thou art a Stranger,* which God gave unto Abraham, *Gen.* 28. 4. Where the very same Word is used concerning *Jacob*, that is expressed in the Prophecy, *Gen.* 5. 13. So that the *Patriarchs* looked on themselves as *Strangers* in the *Land* of Canaan, so long after the *promise* made, and after

G 4 the

the *increase* of the *Seed* of *Abraham*: And therefore the *land* of *Canaan* was called *Terra Peregrinationum*, the *Land* wherein they were *strangers*; *Gen.* 36. 7. -- 37. 1. And when *God* was calling the People of *Israel* together out of *Egypt*, yet then the *Land* of *Canaan* was called by the very same title, the *Land of their Pilgrimage, wherein they were Strangers*: *Exod.* 6. 4. And *Psl.* 105. 9, 10, 11, 12, 13. where we have a full account of the *Promise* made to *Abraham*, *Isaac*, and *Jacob*, concerning the *inheritance* of that *Land* it is said, *that they were few, and Strangers in it, when they went from one Nation to another, from one Kingdom to another People*. Which doth fully explain the meaning of the *Prophecy* in *Genesis*, and that it is not to be restrained to the *servitude*

tude of the *People* of *Israel* in *Egypt*, but to be understood of their state of *Pilgrimage* for 400 Years, wherein they were to suffer great hardships, before they should come to the Inheritance of *Canaan*. *This is no forced or unnatural exposition of the Words*, as you seem to suggest; but to my apprehension, very plain and easie, if we attend to the main scope and design of them which was to acquaint *Abraham* how long it would be before the *prophecy* were accomplished, and what the condition of his Seed should be the mean time, *viz. That they should have no Land which they should call their own by Inheritance all that time, but they should be exposed to great hardships, yea even to Servitude; but that Nation whom they should serve, should at last suffer for*

their

their ill usage of them, and they should come out of that Captivity with great substance; and all this to be done in the fourth Generation of the Amorites *when their Iniquities should be arrived at the full height.* All which particulars, were so remarkably accomplished at such a distance of time, and under such improbable circumstances, that that this very *prophecy* were enough to convince an unprejudiced mind, that it came from Divine Inspiration. For where do we meet with any thing like this in the Histories of other Nations? *viz.* A Prophecy to be accomplished 400 Years after, and the very manner foretold, which no humane conjecture could reach to, since the manner of deliverance of the *People* of *Israel* out of their Captivity in *Egypt*,

Egypt, was to all humane appearance so impossible a thing, especially at such a time when the *Spirits* of the People were sunk and broken by so long a slavery: And not only the manner foretold, but the accomplishment happened to a day, according to *Exodus* 12. 41. *And it came to pass at the end of the* 430 *Years, even the selfe-same day it came to pass, that all the Hosts of the Lord went out from the Land of* Egypt. But against this you object, *That the sojourning is spoken of the Children of* Israel *in* Egypt *for* 430 *Years; which cannot hold good any ways; since, to make it up, the times of* Abraham, Isaac, *and* Jacob, *must be taken in who could not be called the Children of* Israel. *Answ.* For the 430 Years, I grant, that according to St. *Paul,*

they

they did commence from the *Covenant* made to *Abraham* Gal. 3. 17. and that the 400 Years began from *Isaac's* being owned for the *Promised Seed;* between which time the 30 Years were passed; and all appearance of difficulty is avoided, if we admit the reading of the best Copies of the *L X X.* which is in these words, Ἡ δὲ παροικησις τῶν υἱῶν Ἰσραὴλ, ἥν παρῴχησαν ἐν γῇ Αἰγύπτῳ, καὶ ἐν γῇ Χαναὰν, αὐτοὶ καὶ οἱ πατέρες αὐτῶν ἔτη τετρακόσια τριάκοντα, *Now the sojourning of the Children of* Israel *who dwelt in* Egypt *and* Canaan, *they and their Fathers was* 430 *Years.* This is the reading of our *Alexandrian* Copy, and the *Complutensian,* and that of *Aldus,* and of *Eusebius* in his *Chronicon,* and of St. *Hierome* in his Translation of it; and

and of the *Church* in St. *Au-gustins* time, and afterwards; and left any should reject this as a late Interpolation, or gloss received into the Text, besides these Testimonies of the Antiquity of it, we find the very same in the *Samaritan* Copy, which the Enemies of it do allow to be as ancient as our *Saviours* time. And that which very much confirms the Truth of this reading is, that the *Jews* themselves follow the sense of it, who are the most eager contenders for the *Authority* of the *Hebrew* Copy; who all agree, that the beginning of the Computation of the 430 Years is to be taken before the *Children* of *Israels* going into *Egypt*: and *Menasseh Ben Israel* contends with many others, that the 430 Years did begin from

the

the *Promise* made to *Abraham*, and the 400 from the time of *Isaac*, to which their most ancient *Books* of *Chronology* do agree, and to the same purpose speak both *Philo Judæus*, and *Josephus*; who although in one place he seems to make *the* Israelites *affliction in* Egypt *to have been* 400 *Years*, yet when he speaks more particularly of it, *he makes the time of their abode in* Egypt *to have been only* 215, *and the* 430 *to begin from* Abrahams *entrance into* Canaan: The *Targum* of *Jonathan* begins the 430 from the Vision of *Abraham*, and the 400 from the Birth of *Isaac*; all which I mention, to let you see that the *Jews* themselves do in sense concur with the *Samaritan* and *Greek* Copy; and therefore we have more reason to suspect some-

something left out in the present *Hebrew*, than any thing added in those Copies. *But doth not this take off from the Authority of the Scripture?* Not at all: For the only Question is about the True Reading: And having the consent of the *Samaritan*, *Alexandrian*, and other Copies of the *LXX.* and of the Ancient *Church*; and of the *Jews* themselves as to the sense of it, we have reason to look on this as the truer Reading : Which is making no addition to the *scripture* either as to Persons or Places, but only producing the more Authentick Copy; much less is this Adding or Changing as we please, for if we did this without so much Authority as we have for it, you might as easily reject it as we produce it.

3. After

3. After all this, I do not see the mighty force of your Reason to charge the Scripture with Contradiction, supposing *the 400 Years were to be spent in the servitude of the Children of* Israel *in* Egypt. I confess, when I found the *Scripture* so boldly, so frequently charged with no less than Contradiction, I expected something like Demonstration in the Case, especially in this place which you chose to put in the Front of all; but I do not find any thing like such a proof of a Contradiction, supposing we should allow the 400 Years to be spent in *Egypt.* Yes, say you, Coath *was* 5 *Years Old when he came down into* Egypt, *and When he had lived there* 65 *Years he begat* Amram, *and* Amram *being* 70 *Years Old begat* Moses, *to which* Moses *his* 80 *Years being added,*

added, we have only 215 Years.
But since the Scripture doth not
assign, the particular Age of
any of these, when they begat
their Children, I see no impossi-
bility or repugnancy in the supposition, that 400 Years should
pass from *Levi*'s going into *Egypt*,
to the Eightieth of *Moses*, any
more than from *Salmons* entrance
into *Canaan* to the *time* of *David*,
or no more are reckoned in *scrip-*
ture than *Boaz* the Son of *Salmon*,
by *Raab*, and *Obed*, and *Jesse*; So
that by the same way, this lat-
er may be explained, the former may be so too. If it be
said, *That either they begat their*
children at a great Age, or that the
Scripture in Genealogies doth not set
down all the intermediate Parents,
but only the most eminent, (as Caleb
called the Son of Esron.

H.   1 Chron.

1 Chron. 2. 9, 18. *although ther was at leaft one between them,*) the very fame Anfwer will ferve to clear this part of the *Chronology* o *Scripture* from any appearance of Contradiction. Thefe things you might have found more largely deduced and fully handled by thofe Learned Perfons, wh have undertaken to clear the *Chronology* of *Scripture* : Who were men of more Judgment than from any difficulty of thi nature, to call in queftion th *Truth* and *Authority* of the *facre Scriptures*; and although the Opi nions of *Chronologers*, are like th City Clocks, which feldom a gree, yet fome come nearer th time of the day than others do; and therefore you ought to ex amine and compare them befor you pronounce fo peremptorily about

about Contradictions in *scripture*, which you have no reason to do till you find that no one *hypothesis* among them will serve to free the *scripture* from Contradiction: For otherwise, you do but blame the *Sun*, because you cannot make the Clocks agree.

This is all I can find in your Papers under the *head* of Contradictions; and I leave you now soberly to consider, whether this place did afford you sufficient ground for so heavy a Charge; but if you say, *you have a great many more by you, but you sent me this only for a Tryal of my skill;* before you send any more; I beseech you, Sir, to consider,

1. How easily things do appear to be Contradictions to weak, or unstudied, or prejudiced minds, which after due

con-

consideration appear to be no such things. A deep prejudice finds a Contradiction in every thing; whereas in *Truth*, nothing but ill will, and impatience of considering, made any thing, it may be, which they Quarrel at, appear to be so. If I had been of such a quarrelsome humour, I would have undertaken to have found out more Contradictions in your Papers, than you imagin, and yet you might have been confident, you had been guilty of none at all. When I consider the great pains, and Learning, and Judgement, which hath been shewn by the *Christian Writers* in the Explication of the *Scriptures*; and the raw, indigested Objections which some love to make against them, if I were to judge of things barely

by

by the fitneſs of perſons to judge
of them, the diſproportion between theſe, would appear out
of all compariſon. A modeſt
Man would in any thing of this
nature ſay with himſelf, methinks, if there were ſuch Contradictions in the *Bible*, as now
ſeem to me; ſo many perſons of
incomparable Abilities in the
Firſt, and latter Ages of the
Chriſtian Church, who have
made it their buſineſs to enquire
into theſe things, would have
diſcerned them before me: And
yet they retained a mighty vene-
ration for the *ſcriptures*, as com-
ing from God himſelf; and therefore it may be only weakneſs of
Judgement, want of Learning,
or ſome ſecret prejudice may
make me ſuſpect theſe things; or
elſe I muſt ſuſpect the honeſty of

H 3 all

all thofe perfons who have pretended fuch a Devotion to the Scriptures, and yet have believed them full of Contradictions.

2. *Wherein* the Contradiction appears. Is it in the main and weighty parts of the *Religion* revealed herein; or is it only in fome fmaller Circumftances as to time and place? The great thing you are to look after, are the Matters thofe *Scriptures* tell you your Salvation depends upon; and if there be a full confent, and agreement therein; you find enough for you to believe and practice. And if fome Contradictions fhould ftill appear to you in fmaller Matters, what follows from thence, but only that the fame care was not taken about little, as about great things? And you ought to fet that appearance

rance of Contradiction in small
Matters, together with the real
consent in the things of the highest importance; and from thence
rather to infer, that this was no
combination or design to deceive
others; for such persons take the
greatest care to prevent suspicion,
by their exactness in every minute
Circumstance; and sometimes
the over-much care to prevent
suspicion doth raise it the more.

3. *What ways* have been used
by Men of judgement and learning, to clear those places from
the charge of Contradiction.
For, not one of the Objections
you can start now, but hath been
considered over and over; and
all the difficulties that belong to
it examined; If you will not
take the pains to do this; it is
plain you do not desire satisfacti-

on,

on, but only feek for a pretence to cavil; efpecially, if you only fearch the weakeft or moft injudicious Writers on the Scriptures, and endeavour to expofe their opinions, without taking notice of what others have faid with more clear and evident Reafon. This fhews either want of Judgment in choofing fuch Expofitors, or want of Candor and fair dealing and a defire of taking any advantage againft the Scriptures.

4. How hard a Matter it is for us at this diftance to underftand exactly the grounds of *Chronology*, or the manner of computation of Times ufed fo long ago: and therefore in all difficulties of this nature, we ought to make the faireft allowances that may be, confidering with-

withall, that escapes and er-
rours are no where more easily
committed by Transcribers, than
in *numbers*: and that it is a very
unreasonable thing, that a *Book*
otherwise deserving to be
thought the best *Book* in the
World, should be scorned and
rejected, because there appears
some difference in the *computation*
of *times*. We do not so exactly
know the manner of the *Hebrew
Chronology*, nor, the nature of
their Year, or Intercalations,
nor the customs of their *Genealogies*; nor the allowance to be
made for *interregnums*, so as to
be able to define peremptorily in
these things; but it is sufficient
to shew, that there is no impro-
bability in the accounts that are
given; and no sufficient reason
can be drawn from thence to
reject

reject the Authority of the *Scriptures.*

2. I come to consider the places you object, *as containing things inconsistent with the Wisdom, or Goodness of God, according to a rational perswasion*; and those are either, 1. *From the Laws of Moses.* 2. *From the express story of the Bible, or actions of the Prophets.*

1. *From the Laws of Moses*: Your *first Objection* is from *Exod.* 21. 7. *Where a Man is supposed to sell his Daughter; which you say, it is incredible to believe that God should permit; because it implies unnatural affection and covetousness in the Father.* But, Sir, 1. You do not consider, that this is barely a *provisional Law*, and is not the *permission* of the thing, so much as the *regulation* of it, supposing it

to be done, *i. e.* in case a Man
hould part with his interest in
his Daughter to another Person,
upon an extraordinary case of
necessity, as the *Jews* understand
t; yet then, she was not to be
in the condition of a Servant,
but to be either Betrothed to the
Person who receiv'd her, or to
his Son; which was intended for
the restraint of promiscuous Buy-
ng and Selling Daughters, meer-
y for the satisfaction of Lust.
The *Jews* who certainly best understood their own Judicial *Laws*,
do say, that this was never to be
done, but where there was a
presumption of such a *betrothing*;
for no Man could Sell his Daughter to those to whom it was un-
lawful for her to *Marry* by their
Law; so that this was looked on
as a kind of *Espousals* of a young
Girle,

Girle, taken into Wardſhip by another; but ſo, that if ſhe were not Betrothed, ſhe was to remain her 6 Years during her Minority, as the *Jews* underſtand it; unleſs ſhe were redeemed, or ſet Free, or the *Jubile* came, or the Maſter dyed, or the time of her Minority expired.

2. The caſe of *neceſſity* being ſuppoſed, it hath been thought lawful for *Parents* to make advantage by their *Children*, not only by the *Jews*, but by other Nations, who have been in the greateſt eſteem for Wiſdom. For by the *Law* of the 12 *Tables*, among the *Romans*, the *Father* had the liberty of Selling his Son three times, for his own advantage, as *Dionyſ. Halicarnaſſeus* relates; and before that time, it was not only in uſe among the

ie *Romans*, but in such esteem
mong them, that upon the re-
iew of their Laws the *Decem-
ri* durst not leave it out; but
y one of the *Laws* of *Numa
ompilius*, it was restrained to the
mes before Marriage, for in
se the *Son* had the *Fathers* con-
nt to Marry, he could not Sell
m afterwards, as the same
uthor tells us. This *Law* con-
nued in force among them, till
riftianity prevailed in the *Roman
mpire*, for although there were
prohibition of *Diocletian* against
, yet that signified nothing,
l *Constantine* took care, *That
ch indigent Parents should be re-
ved out of the publick charge*, Cod.
heodos. l. 11. tit. 27. 2. And
t after this, the Custom did
ntinue, when the *Parents* were
great want, as appears by a
Law

Law of *Theodoſius*, Cod. 3. tit. 3. *Omnes quos Parentum miſeranda fortuna in ſervitium dum victum requirunt addixit, ingenuitati priſtinæ reformentur.* And it further appears, that even in *Conſtantin's* time, notwithſtanding the Law made by him, *Parents* would ſtill, when they thought themſelves overcharged with Children, part with their Intereſt in them to others for advantage, but it was chiefly while they were *ſanguinolenti*, as the Law expreſſes it, *i. e. new Born.* Cod. *Theod. l. 5. tit.* 8. By the Laws of *Athens*, before *Solons* time, Parents might ſell their Children, as appears by *Plutarch*, in his Life; and the ſame *Philoſtratus* reports of the *Phrygians*, *l.* 3. *vit. Apollon. Tyan.* and the like cuſtom doth obtain among the *Chineſes* to this day

day, if perfons do think themfelves unable to bring up their
Children themfelves.   And there
are two things to be faid for it.
1. The natural obligation lying
on Children to provide for their
Parents in neceffity, by any way
they are able.   2. The probability of better Education under
more able Perfons; and therefore the *Thebans* had a Law, *That
Parents in cafe of poverty, were
to bring their* Children *to the Magi-
ftrate, as foon as they were Born,* Ælian. v.
who put them out to fuch as were judged hift. l. 2. c. 7
*fit to bring them up, and to have
their fervice for their reward.*

But however, you fay, *This
place implys a toleration of having
many Wives, becaufe it is faid, if
he take him another Wife, v.* 10.
I do not deny, that the *Mofaical*
Law did fuppofe the practice of
Poly-

Polygamy; but as it doth no where expresly allow it, neither doth it expresly condemn it. And although we say, the *Christian Law* is far more excellent, which reduceth Marriage to its first institution; yet you will find it a hard Matter to prove such a permission of *Polygamy* as this was, to be so repugnant to the *Law* and Principles of *Nature*, as from thence to infer, that this *Law* of *Moses* could not be from *God*: You might have said the same about the Matter of *Divorce*, which was permitted them; *Christ* saith, *for the hardness of their hearts*: Which shews, that *God* doth not always require that from Men which is best pleasing to himself; and that as to his *Political Government*, he may not always punish that, which is not so pleasing to him.　　The

The next Law you quarrel at
is that, *Deut. 22. 13, &c. About
the tryal of Virginity*: Which you
object against, *as immodest, and
uncertain, and therefore unbecoming
the Wisdom of God*. So, many
customs of those elder times of
the World, and of the *Eastern*
parts to this day seem very
strange to us, that are not so
well acquainted with the *Reasons*
of them. Methinks, it better
becomes our *Modesty* in such ca-
ses, to question our understanding those customes, than presently to cast so much disparage-
ment on the Author of them.
If you had been offended at the
literal sense of those Words, many of the *Jews* themselves say,
they are to be understood figu-
ratively of the evidence that
was to be brought and laid open

I   before

before the *Judges*, on behalf of the defamed Person. And both *Josephus* and *Philo* omit the laying open the Cloth. But supposing it to be taken in the plainest literal sense, I have Two Things to say in vindication of this Law. 1. That however uncertain some *Physitians* have thought that way of Tryal to have been in these parts of the World; yet it is generally agreed to have held for the *Eastern* parts, by the most skilful *Physitians* among the *Arabians*: And a custom of the same nature is said by good Authors to have been observed among the *Egyptians*, and other *Africans*, as well as the *Arabians*; so that this could not be thought so strange or immodest among the Inhabitants of those parts: And it is very probable that some

par-

particulars, as to the Practice of these *Laws* are not set down, which might very much tend to the certainty of them, as the Age of the Married Persons, which was most likely then, as it is to this day in the *Eastern* parts, very early, the *Jews* say, at 12 years old, which would make the Tryal more certain. 2. As to the Modesty of it, you are to consider, that the *Law* was intended to keep persons from unjust *defamations*, and such a way of *Tryal* was therefore pitched upon to deter persons from such defamations; which Men might otherwise have been more ready to, because of the *liberty* of *divorce*, and the advantage they had in saving the *dower*, if they could prove the party vitiated before Marriage; therefore all the proof

I 2   of

of that Nature was to be passed soon after the consummation of Marriage, which being agreed then by all the Friends, there was to be no liberty left for defamation afterwards; but in case any Man should be guilty of it, the producing those Evidences, which before they were agreed upon, should be sufficient to clear the Innocency of the party accused. And therefore I look on this *Law*, as the *Jews* do on that of the *rebellious son*, of which they say, that there is no instance of the practice of it; the Penalty threatned being so effectual to prevent the occasion of it.

And such in a great Measure, I suppose the other *Law* mentioned by you to have been, *viz.* *of the Water of Jealousy*, which you make so strange a matter of; and

and think it *favours too much of a design to gratify the jealous humour of the Jewish Nation*: But you might have put a fairer construction upon it, *viz.* That it was intended to prevent any occasion of suspicion being given to the Husband, by too much familiarity with other persons ; since the Law allowed so severe a Trial, in Case the Wife after admonition did not forbear such suspected familiarity, but if you had looked on the Law, as it is, Num. 5. 12, 13. &c. you would have found, that the design of it was to keep Women from committing *secret Adultery*, by so severe a Penalty; yet withall allowing so much to a reasonable suspicion, (for so the *Jews* understand it, with many Cautions and Limitations) that rather

I 3   then

then Married perfons fhould live under perpetual jealoufies, he appointed this extraordinary way of Tryal, whereby Adultery was moft feverely punifhed, and the honour of Innocency publickly vindicated; which certainly are not ends at all unbecoming due Conceptions of God.

The laft of the *Jewifh Laws*, which you quarrel with is *the prohibition of Ufury, in feveral places of Mofes his Law and the Pfalms:* And from hence you fall into a long Difcourfe *to prove the lawfulnefs of Ufury:* But to what purpofe I befeech you? For you were to prove, that *God* could never forbid it; you might have spared *your pity for Men*, as you think, *Blinded with fuperftition, and cheated with New and Aëry Notions:* For by all that I can fee by thefe

Papers,

Papers, some pretended Enemies to *superstition* have no better Eyes than their Neighbours, and are as easily cheated with groundless Fancies and Aëry imaginations. The only thing to the business in that long Discourse is this, *That you cannot imagine that God should make a Law so much to Mans inconvenience, and forbid him so nice and indifferent a thing, as Moderate increase of profit by letting out of Money, when it is allowed upon Lands, Houses, and Trade,* &c. To this I Answer, that the prohibition of *Usury*, to the *Jewish Nation*, was upon *political Grounds* peculiar to the constitution of that *People;* as appears by the words of the Law, *Deut.* 23. 19, 20. *Thou shalt not lend to Usury unto thy Brother* ---- *Unto a Stranger thou maist lend upon Usury;* but

I 4   none

none of the *Laws* which are foun-
ded upon common and Moral
Reasons have such Limitations
as this; for God would never
have said, *Thou shalt not commit
Adultery with thy Brothers Wife*; but
*with the Wife of a Stranger thou
maist.* But there was this particular Reason, for the prohibition of *Usury* to the *Jewish Nation*:
It pleased God to fix their Habi-
tation, not upon the Sea-side,
as *Tyre* and *Sidon* stood; but
within Land where they had no
conveniencies of Trading, but
the Riches of the *Nation* lay in
Agriculture and *Pasturage*: In
which the Returns of Money are
neither so quick nor so advantageous to make sufficient compensa-
tion for the Interest of the Money
in the time they have it: For the
main thing valuable in Money is
the

the advantage the borrower
makes of it; and where that is
great, it seems reasonable that the
person whose the Money is, should
have a proportionable share of the
advantage made by it; but where
persons borrow only for present
occasions to supply their necessities, there it is only an Act of kind-
ness to lend, and it would be unreasonable to press upon, or take
advantage by anothers necessities.
And this seems to have been the
case among the *Jews*; they were only the Poor that wanted Money for
present necessities; the Rich had
no way to imploy it in Trading,
unless that they lent to the *Tyrian
Merchants*, which it was lawful
by their Law to do; now if they
took *Usury* of their own people,
it must be of those whose urgent
necessity, and not hopes of a
mighty

mighty increafe by it made them borrow, and therefore it was a very juft and reafonable *Law* to forbid *Ufury* among them : which I believe he would never have done, if he had placed the *Jews* upon the Coafts of *Phœnicia*, where Trading was fo much in requeft.

Thefe are all the *Laws* which you have picked out of the *whole* Body of the *Jewifh Law*, to reprefent it unbecoming the *Wifdom* of *God*: And now I pray Sir, look back again upon them, fee how few, how fmall, how weak your Objections are; and compare them with the *weight*, and *juftice*, and *prudence*, and *piety*, exprefled in all the reft, and I hope you will find caufe to be afhamed of fpeaking fo har-fhly of thofe *Laws*, fo well

acco-

accommodated to those Ages of the World, and the Condition of that *People* for whom they were appointed.

2. I now consider what you object against the *story* of the *Bible.*

1. *That passage of* Moses, Exod. 32. 32. *Blot me out of thy Book which thou hast written :* Where your design is to shew that Moses *prayed to be Damned, and that this was a very irrational thing : And favouring more of paffism than of the Spirit of God.* But what if *Moses* meant no such thing as Damnation? As there is not any word in the Context relating that ways, but all the design of that Chapter is about a Temporal punishment, which was a present Destruction of the People for their sins. And the Book out of which he prayed

God

God to blot him, feems to me to be no other, than the Roll of *Gods chofen people, who were to poffefs the Land of* Canaan: For fo ספר properly fignifies a *Roll* or *Register*. *Pfalm* 69. 28. We meet with ספר חיום *the Roll of the living, or the Book of the living* we render it, becaufe all ancient *Books* were in the fafhion of *Rolls*. In that Chapter, *Mofes* intercedes with *God* on behalf of the People, that he would make good his promife to them, of bringing them into the *Land of* Canaan. *v.* 13. and *v.* 30. He goes up to make an Atonement for the People, i. e. *as to the cutting them off in the Wildernefs*, and therefore he defires rather than the People fhould be deftroy'd, *that God would ftrike him out of the Roll, that he might Dye in the*

the Wildernefs rather than the People : And God gives that Anfwer to this purpofe , v. 33. *Whoever hath finned againft me , will I blot out of my Book*, the fenfe of which is the fame with thofe words of the *Pfalmift , he fware in his wrath that they fhould not enter into his Reft.* *Pfal.* 95, 11. And according to this interpretation, which is moft natural and eafie, all your long Difcourfe *againft praying to be Damned* comes to juft nothing ; there being no pretence for it, either in the Text or Context.

2. The *ftory* of *Ruth* doth not pleafe you , *as favouring in your opinion of a great deal of Immodefty ;* but you would have a better opinion of it, if you confider that the reafon of her carriage towards *Boaz*, in fuch a manner , was upon *Naomies* telling her *that*

he

he was one to whom the right of re-
demption did belong, and by confe-
quence, by their Law, *was to*
Marry her. Ruth 2. 20. And
this Ruth pleaded to Boaz,
Ruth 3. 9. By which it appears,
that she verily believed that he
was *legally* her Husband; and
Boaz we see speaks of her *as one*
that was a vertuous Woman, and
known to be such in the whole City.
v. 11. And he confesses *he was*
her near kinsman, only he saith,
there was one nearer. v. 12. By
which it seems, if there had not,
Boaz had made no Scruple of
the matter: And the *Jews* say,
in such Marriages very little *Cere-*
mony was required, if the next
of *kin* did not renounce his right,
because the *Law* had determined
the *Marriage* before hand. If
you had but considered this one
thing,

hing, you would have spared
he many *Observations* you make
on this story.

3. You Object against *2 Sam.*
12. 8. *as too much countenancing
either Inceſt or Adultery, becauſe it
s ſaid, that God gave to* David *his
Maſters Wives into his Boſom.* But
1. It is very ſtrange to bring this
place as a countenance to *Adultery,*
vhich was purpoſely deſigned to
upbraid *David* with the ſin of
Adultery; and you will find it
no eaſie matter, by the conſti-
ution of the *Moſaical Law,*
o prove *Polygamy* to be
Adultery. 2. The *Jews* give a
air Interpretation of this place,
or they ſay, that the *Wife* of a
King could never *Marry* after her
Husbands deceaſe, as the *Gemara*
on the Title *Sanhedrim* expreſly
ſaith, although ſome among
them

them follow the opinion of *R. Jehuda*, that she might Marry the succeeding *King*; but that is built chiefly on this place; of which the rest give a better account, *viz.* that ⬛⬛⬛ doth not imply *Sauls Wives*, but the *Maids of Honour*, or *Attendants*, on the *Court* of *Saul*, which all fell into *Davids* power, and out of whom he might choose *Wives*, without danger of *Incest*; and even some of those who assert it lawful for one *King* to Marry his predecessors Wife, yet say in this case of *David*, that the Word only implies, that they were of *Saul's* Family, as *Merab* and *Michal* were, but not *Saul's Wives*. So that all the difficulty here arises only from the Interpretation of an *unusual word*, in which we have much more reason to trust the

Selden. vxor Ebra. l.1.c.10. Schick. De jure Reg. c. 16. Theor. 19.

the *Jews* than other Writers.

4. You are much offended *at Hosea's Marrying an Adulteress*: But all the formidable difficulties of that place will presently vanish, if you allow the *Prophetical Schemes*, wherein those things are said to be done, which are intended only to represent in a more lively manner the things signified by them. And so you may see the *Chaldee Paraphrase*, fully explains this place of *Hosea* and *Maimonides* purposely discourseth on the *Prophetick parables*, and brings this as one of the instances of them; and with him the rest of the *Jewish Interpreters* agree: But you Object against such a way of Teaching, *as tending to the encouragement of Vice*, which it is very far from, being designed to represent the odiousness of it:

Maim. Moro Nevoch. l. c. 46.

K   For

For the whole Scope of the *Prophet* is to let the People understand, that their *Idolatry* was as hateful to *God* as the sin of *Adultery*, and that the consequence of it would be their Misery and Ruine. And yet that *God* expressed as much tenderness to them, as a Man that was very fond of a Woman would do, in being unwilling to put her away, although he knew she were false to his Bed: the former is intended in the first *Chapter*, and the latter in the third. And what is there tending to Immorality in all this? May not *God* make use of one Vice, whose evil is more notorious to represent another by, whose evil they are more hardly convinced of? May not he set forth a *Degenerate People* by the *Sons* of an *Adulteress*? And by the Names

given

given to them expreſs his deteſta-
tion of their wickedneſs? Eſpe-
cially when the *Parabolical* Terms
are ſo clearly explained, as
they are in the ſecond Chapter.

But you will ſay, *theſe things
are related as plain matters of Fact:
with the ſeveral circumſtances belonging to them.* It is true, they
are ſo, but ſo Parables uſe to be;
ſo was *Nathan's* to *David;* ſo is
that of the Rich Man and *Laza-
rus* in the *New Teſtament;* ſo is *Jer. 13. 4, 5.*
Jeremies going to *Euphrates to hide
his Girdle;* (for it is not very likely
the *Prophet* ſhould be ſent 18 or
20 days Journey into an Enemies
Country for no other end:) So
is *Ezekiels lying on one ſide for* 390 *Ezek. 4. 5, 6*
days, and having his Head and
Beard contrary to the Law, as *Ezek. 5. 1.*
Maimonides obſerves: And his

K 2 *digging*

digging in the *Walls* of the *Temple* at Hierusalem, while he was in *Babylon*: And many other things of a like nature, which are set forth with as punctual a Narration of circumstances as this of *Hosea*, and yet they were only figurative expressions. We that are accustomed to another way of Learning, think these things strange; but this was a very common way in the *elder* times, and it is to this day much used in the *Eastern Countries*, to represent *Duties* to some, under the *Parables* of things as really done by others: As may be seen in *Locman* and *Perzoes*, besides what *Clemens Alexandrinus* and others have said, concerning the *Antiquity* and common use of this *Parabolical* way of Teaching.

I now come to your Objections

ons against the *New Testament*: but I find them so few, and those so slight and inconsiderable, as to the end for which you produce them, that I may easily pass them over. To that *about the continuance of Miracles*, I have already Answer'd: And I find not one word in the places mentioned by you, which implies the necessity of the continuance of them in all Ages of the *Christian Church*. That place, *Mark* 10. 29, 30. speaks of no more but such a *recompence* in this life *as is consistent with persecution*; and therefore must chiefly lie in inward contentment; which all wise Men have valued above external accommodations; although withall, by the account St. *Paul* gives of himself, and his Brethren,

thren, God did abundantly provide for them one way or other.
*As having nothing, and yet enjoying
all things* : Which amounts to
a Hundred-fold in this life.

But certainly you are the firſt
Man, Who have Objected *the
obſcurity of the Book of Revelations, againſt the Authority of the
Scriptures* : Which is juſt as if
one ſhould Object the *quadra-
ture* of the *Circle* againſt
Mathematical certainty. If we
grant that there are ſome things
in that *Myſtical Book*; we do
not yet well underſtand; what
then! Muſt neither that *Book*,
nor any other of the *Bible* be
of *Divine Revelation?* I will
not purſue the unreaſonable-
neſs of this way of arguing ſo
far as I might; but I leave your
ſelf to conſider of it; and of
all

all that I have Written, in order to your *satisfaction*. If you think fit to return an Answer, I pray do it clearly and shortly, and with that freedom from Passion, which becomes so weighty a Matter : And I beseech *God* to give you a right understanding in all things. I am

June 11.
1675.

Sir,

Your Faithful Servant.

FINIS.

Books sold by Moses Pitt, at the Angel in St. Paul's Church-Yard.

Folio.

Theses Theologicæ variis Temporibus in Academia *Sedanensi* editæ, & ad disputandum propositæ. Authore *Ludovico le Blanc* verbi Divini Ministro & Theologiæ professore. In qua exponitur sententia Doctorum Ecclesiæ Romanæ, & Protestantium. Price 20 *s.*

Dr. *Henry Hammond's* Sermons. 1675.

A Table of Ten thousand Square Numbers, by *John Pell*, D.D. stitcht, 1 *s.* 6 *d.*

Tuba Stentoro-Phonica, or the Speaking-Trumpet; being an Instrument of excellent use both at Sea and Land; by Sir *Samuel Morland.* Price of the Book 1 *s.* of the Instrument 2 *l.* 5 *s.*

Articles and Rules for the Government of His Majesties Forces by Land, during this present War, 1673. 1 *s.* 6 *d.*

Bailii opus Hist. Chronol. vet. & Nov. Test. 1663.

Becmanni Exercitationes Theol. Contra Socinianos.

An History of the Church, by *Alex. Petrey.* 1662.

Catalogus Librorum in Regionibus Transmarinis nuper Editorum. *Quarto.*

Quarto.

Dr. *Pell's* Introduction to *Algebra.* 7 *s.*

Nich. Mercatoris Logarithmo-Technia, five methodus conftruendi Logarithmos, 1668. & *Jac. Gregorii* Exercitationes Geometricæ, 1668. 2 *s.*

Love only for Love fake, a Dramatick Romance, by Sir *Richard Fanfhaw.* 3 *s.* 6 *d.*

Mori Enchiridion Metaphyficum, 1671. 10 *s.*

Snellii Typhis Batavus, Ludg. Bat. 1624. 5 *s.*

Petrus Paaw de Offibus, Amft. 1633. 5 *s.*

Dr. *Thomas Jacomb,* on the Eighth Chapter of the *Romans.* 8 *s.*

A Letter from a Gentleman of the Lord *Howard's* Retinue, to his Friend in *London,* dated at *Fez, Nov.* 1. 1670. 6 *d.*

Dr. *Wallis* Opera Mechanica, 22 *s.*

Hieronymi Mercurialis de Arte Gymnaftica, Libri fex cum figuris, 1672.

Pignorii Menfa Ifaica, 1669.

Pharmacopeia ⎰Hagienfis, 1659.
⎱Auguftana, 1672.

J. Crellii Ethica Ariftotelica & Chriftiana, 16 *s.*

Joan. Binchii Mellificium Theologicum, 16 *s.*

Theod. Kerkringii D. M. *Spicilegium Anatomicum,* Continens Obfervationum Anatomicarum rariorum centuriam unam nec non Ofteogeniam fœtuum in qua quid cuique officulo fingulis accedat Menfibus, quidve decedat & in eo per varia immutetur tempora, accuratiffime oculis fubjiciuntur, 1670.

There

There is newly publiſhed two *Recantation-Sermons* (Preached at the *French*-Church in the *Savoy*) by two Converted *Romaniſts*, Mr. *De la Motte*, late Preacher of the Order of the *Carmelites*; and Mr. *De Luzanzy*, Licentiate in Divinity; wherein the Corrupt Doctrines of the Church of *Rome* are laid open and confuted. Both Printed in *French* and *Engliſh*.

Alſo two other Sermons, one Preached before the King at *White-Hall*, *Jan*. 30. 1676. by *Henry Eagſhaw*, D. D. the other before the Lord Mayor, Dec. 19. 1675. by *John Cook*.

A Modeſt Survey of the moſt material things in a diſcourſe, called the *Naked Truth*, 6 *d*.

Octavo.

A diſcourſe of *Local Motion*, undertaking to demonſtrate the Laws of Motion, and withall to prove, that of the ſeven Rules delivered by Mr. *Des Cartes* on this Subject, he hath miſtaken Six: Engliſhed out of *French*, 1671.   1 *s*.

The Hiſtory of the late Revolution of the Empire of the Great *Mogol*, with a deſcription of the Countrey, in two Volumes. 7 *s*.

The Hiſtory of the Conqueſt of the Empire of *China* by the *Tartars*. 1671. 4 *s*.

Myſtery of Iniquity unvailed in a diſcourſe, wherein is held forth the oppoſition of the Doctrine, Worſhip, and Practices of the *Roman* Church, to the Nature, Deſigns, and Characters of the Chriſtian Faith, by *Gilbert Burnet*. 1 *s*.

A Collection of *Popiſh Miracles* wrought by Popiſh Saints, both during their lives, and after their death, collected out of their own Authors, 1 *s*.   *Theod*.

Theod. Turqueti, De Mayerne, De Arthritide, Accesserunt ejusdem Consilia aliquot Medicinalia, 1 *s.*

A new way of curing the Gout, and Observations and Practices relating to Women in Travel, 3 *s.*

A Relation of a Conference held about Religion at *London, Apr.* 3. 1676. by *Edward Stillingfleet,* D.D. and *Gilbert Burnet,* with some Gentlemen of the Church of *Rome.* 2 *s.* 6 *d.*

Elenchi Motuum Nuperorum in Anglia pars tertia, sive Motus Compositi. Ubi G. Monchii *e Scotia progressus, nec non* Aug. Caroli Secundi *in Angliam Reditus; ejusdemq; Regiæ Majest. per Decennium gesta fideliter enarrantur,* 1676.

Gualteri Needham Disputatio Anatomica de Formato Fœtu. 1667. 3 *s.* 6 *d.*

Buxtorfius's Epitome of his *Hebrew* Grammar Englished, by *John Davis,* 1658. 1 *s.* 6 *d.*

The *Fortunate Fool,* or the Life of Dr. *Cenudo,* a *Spanish* Romance, 1670. 2 *s.*

The Adventures of Mr. *T. S.* an *English* Merchant, taken Prisoner by the *Turks* of *Argiers,* with a description of that Kingdom, and the Towns and Places thereabouts, 1670. 1 *s.* 6 *d.*

Contemplations on Mortality, 1670. 1 *s.*

A Discourse written to a Learned Frier, by Mr. *Des Fourneillis,* shewing that the Systeme of Mr. *Des Cartes,* and particularly his Opinion concerning Brutes, does contain nothing dangerous; and that all he hath written of both, seems to have been taken

out

but of the First Chapter of *Genesis* : To which is annexed the *Systeme General* of the *Cartesian* Philosophy, 1 *s.*

The Relation of a Voyage into *Mauritania* in *Africk*, by *Roland Frejus* of *Marseilles*, by the French Kings order, 1666, to *Muley Arxid* King of *Taffaletta*, &*c.* with a Letter in Answer to divers Questions concerning their Religion, Manners, &*c.* 1671. 1 *s.* 6 *d.*

A Genuine Explication of the Visions in the Book of *Revelation*, by *A. B. Peganius.* 1671. 2 *s.*

Prodromus to a Dissertation concerning Solids naturally contained within Solids, laying a foundation for the rendring a rational account, both of the Frame and the several Changes of the Mass of the Earth, as also the various Productions of the same. By *Nich. Steno*, 1671. 1 *s.* 3 *d.*

Basilius Valentinus, of Natural and Supernatural things, also of the first Tincture, Root, and Spirits of Metals and Minerals, how the same are Conceived, Generated, Brought forth, Changed and Augmented : Whereunto is added *Frier Bacon* of the Medicine or Tincture of Antimony, Mr. *John Isaack Holland* his works of *Saturn*, and *Alexander Van Suchten*, of the Secrets of Antimony out of *Dutch*, 1671. 2 *s.*

The Poetical Histories, being a compleat Collection of all the Stories necessary for a perfect understanding of the Greek and Latin Poets, and other Ancient Authors, written
Originally

Originally in *French*, by the Learned Jesuite *P. Galtruchius*. Now *Englished* and Enriched with Observations concerning the Gods worshiped by our Ancestors in this Island, by the *Phœnecians* and *Syrians* in *Asia*; with many useful Notes and occasional Proverbs, gathered out of the best Authors: Unto which are added two Treatises; One of the Curiosities of Old Rome, and of the difficult Names relating to the Affairs of that City; The other containing the most remarkable Hieroglyphicks of *Egypt*. The Third Edition, with Additions. By *Marius D' Assigny*, B. D. 3 *s.* 6 *d.*

An *Essay* about the Origine and Virtues of Gems, by the Honourable *Robert Boyle*. 1 *s.* 6 *d.* Idem Lat. *twelves*, 1 *s.*

Sir *Samuel Morland*'s Arithmetick, with several useful Tables, and a Perpetual Almanack, 1673. 3 *s.*

A Compleat Treatise of Chyrurgery, containing *Barbetts* Chirurgery. *Mindererus* of Diseases Incident to Camps and Fleets: With a Chyrurgeons Chest of *Medicines* and *Instruments*. &c. 6 *s.*

Dr. *Lower* de corde. *Amster.* 1671. 3 *s.*

Dr. *Grews* Anatomy of Vegetables, 1672. 2 *s.*

Crowei Elenchi Script. in Scripturam. 3 *s.* 6 *d.*

Engelenus de Scorbuto.

Fred. Deckeri Exercitationes Medicæ.

Grotii viâ ad Pacem.

Alb.

Alb. Gentilis de Armis Romanis.
    De Imperio.
    De Legationibus.
    De Nuptiis.
Hammond de Confirmatione.
Hugenii momenta Defultoria.
Parai Chronologia Sacra.
Thrufton de Refpiratione.
      Twelves.
A *Paradife of Delights,* or an *Elixir* of
Comforts offered to *Believers,* in two difcour-
fes, the firft on *Heb.* 6. 17, 18. the fecond
on *Rom.* 8. 32. By *Robert Wyne.* 1 *s.*
Grotii Sophompaneas.
Gronovius in Livium.
Primrofe Ars Pharmaceutica.
Schook de Pace.
Suetonius.
Swalve Alcali.
Severini Synopfis Chyrurgiæ.
Terentii Flores.
Trelcatii loci Communes.
Balduinus de *Calceo* & *Nigronius* de *Caliga
Veterum.* Accefferunt ex *Q. Sept. Fl. Tertulli-
ani,* Cl. *Salmafii* & *Alb. Rubenii* Scriptis pluri-
ma ejufdem Argumenti, 1667.
    Pauli Barbetti opera Chirurgica Anato-
mica, 1672.
    Praxis *Barbettiana* Cum notis *Fred. Deckeri,
Ottonis Tachenii* Hippocrates Chymicus,
    Q. Horatii Poemata cum Commentariis Jo.
Menellii, 1676.
    Hugo Grotius de veritate Religionis Chrifti-
anæ, 1674.
                   Theo-

Theodori Kerckringii D. M. Commentarius in *Currum Triumphalem Antimonii Basilii Valentini* a se latinitate donatum, 1671.

Jo. Pincieri M. D. Ænigmatum Libri Tres cum solutionibus, 1655.

Francisci Redi Experimenta circa res diversas naturales, speciatim illas quæ ex Indiis adseruntur, 1675.

Aulus Gellius.

Besterfeldus Redivivus.

Herls Wisdoms *Tripos.*

Wilkins Beauty of Providence.

Quarto.

A New Dictionary, *French* and *English*, by *Guy Miege.* 1677.

Marshal *Turenne's* Funeral Sermon. 1677.

Jer. Horroccii. Angl. Opusc. Astron. 1673.

An Historical Vindication of the Church of *England* in Point of Schism, by Sir *Ro. Twisden.*

The last Siege of *Mastricht. Sept.* 5. 1676.

Dr. *Tillotson's* Sermon before the King, *Apr.* 18. 1675.

Dr. *Wilkins's* two Sermons before the King, *March* 7. 1669. and *Feb.* 7. 1670.

Dr. *Jo. Tillotson's* Rule of Faith. 1676.

Rhetores selecti: Demetrius Phalerius, Tiberius Rhetor, Anonymus Sophista, Severus Alexandrinus Grecè et Lat. per Tho. Gale. *Soc. Coll.* M. 1676.

A Scriptural Catechism, according to the Method observed by the Author of the *Whole Duty of Man*, 1676.

How., of delighting in God; of the blessedness of the Righteous. Two Vol.

Art of Speaking, by *M. du Port-Royal,* 1676.

CPSIA information can be obtained at www.ICGtesting.com

230711LV00003B/27/P